As Director of an evangelical outreach ministry to lesbian anu gay people, I am constantly reminded of the way that church teachings on homosexuality have caused immense damage to human lives and relationships. With superb clarity of style and presentation, Dr Sharpe successfully demonstrates in The Gay Gospels *that these harsh teachings have no basis either in the Bible or in the mission of our Lord and Saviour, Jesus Christ. This book will be of enormous value to all involved in the debate over homosexuality and Christianity currently raging in the church and wider society.*

Jeremy Marks, Director of Courage UK

Do you think that the Bible condemns LGBT people for wanting loving and intimate relationships with people of their own sex? At the London Lighthouse AIDS hospice it was evident that such homophobic distortion can and does blight lives. This humane and scholarly book helps us to a truer understanding of God's love for all human beings, and how those insights developed in the history of the Christian faith, chronicled in the Bible.

Andrew Henderson, Founding Co-chair of London Lighthouse

This is a must-read for all LGBT people, and is definitely Good News. I couldn't put it down. Through exhaustive research, Dr Sharpe exposes the hypocrisy and cant of the anti-gay elements within the Christian church past and present by placing the Biblical evidence in its proper context of an ancient society obsessed by procreation, and a Jesus who was certainly pro-gay and perhaps even gay himself. It is full of Revelations and, armed with its evidence, the LGBT community can now move confidently forward towards its own Resurrection within the Christian church.

Robert Orledge, Emeritus Professor, University of Liverpool

In recent years the LGBT community has come under sustained attack from Christian leaders. This book will equip gay people to defend themselves against what Dr Sharpe shows convincingly is totally unjustified condemnation. In particular, the chapters on Jesus' lifestyle offer a vision of Christianity full of hope for LGBT people.
James Ledward, Editor of Gscene magazine

In this polemical work Dr Sharpe presents a provocative and illuminating view of the radical and transfiguring character of Christ's mission, and analyses its implications in the context of the current debate in the Church about human sexuality. The book is written in coherent, assured and accessible prose, and the arguments are refreshing, invigorating and persuasive.
Father William Davage

With its unique combination of defensive and affirmative arguments this important book lays bare the impoverished ideology which is the real foundation of Christian homophobia. It makes an extremely valuable contribution to the collapsing taboo against homosexuality.
Colin Coward, Director, Changing Attitude England

The Gay Gospels

Good News for LGBT People

The Gay Gospels

Good News for LGBT People

Keith Sharpe

BOOKS

Winchester, UK
Washington, USA

First published by O-Books, 2011
O-Books is an imprint of John Hunt Publishing Ltd., Laurel House, Station Approach,
Alresford, Hants, SO24 9JH, UK
office1@o-books.net
www.o-books.com

For distributor details and how to order please visit the 'Ordering' section on our website.

Text copyright: Keith Sharpe 2010

ISBN: 978 1 84694 548 9

A CIP catalogue record for this book is available from the British Library.

Design: Stuart Davies

Printed in the UK by CPI Antony Rowe
Printed in the USA by Offset Paperback Mfrs, Inc

We operate a distinctive and ethical publishing philosophy in all
areas of our business, from our global network of authors to
production and worldwide distribution.

CONTENTS

Introduction: The Purpose of this Book

The four gospels of the Bible's New Testament bring the Good News of Christ's salvation to 'all mankind'. For many lesbian, gay, bisexual and transgendered (LGBT) people, however, the good news has had a hard job getting through.

Over the past two millenia the mainstream patriarchal Christian churches charged with transmitting the gospel message have been the main obstacle to LGBT people hearing any good news at all. These churches have rigidly imposed a rule of compulsory heterosexuality and condemned LGBT people as wicked, evil and intrinsically disordered. They assume that men and women are all naturally heterosexual and that homosexual behaviour is therefore just heterosexuals behaving badly. This unwarranted assumption has justified the persecution and cruel punishments of the past and the discrimination and exclusion of the present.

These patriarchal churches have scoured the pages of the Bible in search of textual buttressing for their prejudice, and have come up with a handful of isolated verses.

These few references in fact provide extremely doubtful support. During the past thirty years scholarly scrutiny of the so-called 'texts of terror' (Phyllis Trible 2003) – for that is how they have been used in the intimidation of LGBT people – has revealed them to be seriously wanting as anything approaching a clear biblical repudiation of same sex love.

At the same time these churches have passed over in silence the passages in the Bible which appear to affirm and celebrate homoerotic desire and relationships. More recent research has begun to bring these to light and in so doing rescue the Bible from the unrelenting homophobia which sadly so many Christian leaders claim to see in it.

This book is designed as a self-help manual for LGBT people

in the face of continuing attacks by Christian leaders. It is also an epistle for LGBT people, urging that the baby not be thrown out with the bathwater. It takes seriously the promise in St John's gospel: *For God so loved the world that he gave his only begotten Son, that whosoever believeth in him should not perish, but have everlasting life.* John 3:16.

This promise is for all God's children, not just the heterosexual ones.

The Good News which I hope these Gay Gospels will bring is divided in two testaments.

The **Defensive Testament** analyses the meaning of each of the 'terror texts' in turn to demonstrate that they have in fact nothing to do with homosexuality as we know it. The cumulative message of this testament is that there is no condemnation of same sex love to be found anywhere in the Bible.

The **Affirmative Testament** uncovers open and hidden affirmations of LGBT lives in the Bible. The cumulative message of this testament is that there are celebrations of same sex love to be found in many books of the Bible.

This is therefore a practical book with pragmatic purposes. Although it draws on scholarly research in pursuing these purposes it is not in itself an academic work. Its aim is to make the findings of contemporary Biblical research better known, especially amongst the LGBT community. Hopefully the reader will find its format and style easy and accessible. Short biblical texts are directly quoted, but always in context and solely in order to show what is actually there to be seen if only eyes would be opened.

At the end of each chapter in both Testaments there is a short summary of key points. These set out the main arguments for LGBT people to deploy in self-defence and in self-affirmation when debating with Christians seeking to deny them equal human rights.

Some people may find it useful to learn these arguments by

heart. Whilst great strides have been made over recent decades in recognising in law the humanity of LGBT people, it remains a regrettable fact that the patriarchal Christian churches continue to be the main source of legitimation for those who oppose equality and who support discrimination against gay people. This book is therefore very relevant to people who are not religious, because the Christian churches still exert a strong influence over social policy, legislation and public opinion. It is vitally important that every opportunity be taken to remind these churches that their endorsement of homophobia is illegitimate in the eyes of the one in whose name they claim to speak and who came so that all, not just some, might be saved.

www.thegaygospels.com

Acknowledgements

I should like to thank all the friends and colleagues who in many and various ways have supported me in the writing of this book. I am grateful to Dr Ruth Cowl of the Open University for help in researching chapter A11. I would like also to put on record my admiration for the theological scholars whose work is described and cited in the text. Thanks to their creativity and insight, the ideological bias of so much church teaching is being unmasked, and thereby the essential inclusiveness of a supposedly anti-gay Bible is being significantly recovered. In particular I would like to pay special tribute to the work of Theodore W Jennings Jr, whose brilliant exegesis of both Old and New Testaments has revealed the extent to which homoerotic sentiment runs through the entire Bible. His seminal and groundbreaking work permeates the analysis offered here, especially in the Affirmative Testament. I hope that this book will further popularise Jennings' enormous contribution to contemporary Biblical scholarship, and in so doing help to achieve his aim, stated in the preface to his excellent book, 'Jacob's Wound', of 'relieving the wholly unwarranted spiritual agony' that afflicts so many gay Christians worldwide.

The Defensive Testament Chapter D1

The Story of Sodom

Sodomites

I invite you to think about the word 'sodomite'. It may have a slightly old fashioned ring but consider how potent the word 'sodomite' still is. To be a sodomite is to be a complete outcast. To be a sodomite is to be the epitome of evil and wickedness, utterly deserving of God's wrathful vengeance, punishment and annihilation. The word even now is virtually unspeakable.

People feel uncomfortable hearing or seeing it.

People believe that 'sodomite' means homosexual.

People believe that Sodom and Gomorrah were destroyed by God because the 'Sodomites' who lived there indulged in homosexual practices. People believe this because it is what the Christian churches have told them.

But there are strong grounds for believing that what the Christian churches have told them is not true.

Abraham's hospitality is rewarded

The story starts in Genesis chapter 18 with God appearing to Abraham mysteriously in the form of three strangers. Abraham's response to the strangers' unexpected arrival is to be extraordinarily welcoming: *When he saw them, he ran to meet them from the tent door, and bowed himself toward the ground'*. Genesis 18:2.

He then invites them in and tells his wife to give them the very best food in the house. In the Genesis verses we are given a lot of details about just how wonderful this food is. The strangers are not just to be fed but to be offered a royal feast.

Abraham is the very model of humility and hospitality. And because of this the strangers tell him that he is to be rewarded with the promise that his wife will bear him a son, despite the fact that both of them are *'old and well stricken in age'*.

Two of the strangers set out for Sodom

Two of the men then leave for the town of Sodom. The one remaining identifies himself as the Lord and explains that he has sent the other two, who are angels appearing as men, to find out if the town of Sodom is really as wicked as he has heard.

There then follows a fascinating conversation between Abraham and the remaining stranger, the Lord. Abraham asks if everybody in Sodom will be destroyed if it is found to be truly wicked. He is concerned that the righteous will perish with the wicked. There could for example be fifty righteous men. Surely it is not right that they should be killed alongside the unrighteous? The Lord agrees he would spare Sodom if fifty righteous men could be found there. But suppose there were only forty-five? asks Abraham. No, the Lord would spare the city if there were forty-five righteous men. Abraham pushes the point. Forty? Thirty? Twenty? Ten? The Lord agrees that Sodom would not be destroyed if there are ten righteous men. Notice though that the concern of both Abraham and the Lord is only with men. Neither seems bothered that all the women might be righteous and yet will be destroyed.

Lot's hospitality and the Sodomites' inhospitality

In Sodom the two strangers are greeted by Lot, Abraham's nephew, who is not a citizen of Sodom, but a resident alien. Just like his uncle, Lot is extremely welcoming and respectful towards these men he does not know: *Lot seeing them, rose up to met them; and he bowed himself with his face toward the ground.* Genesis 19:1

And also like his uncle, Lot is a generous host and after feeding them handsomely offers to give them both beds for the night. But at this point all the townsmen of Sodom surround Lot's house and demand: *Where are the men who came to you tonight?*

Bring them out to us that we may know them. Genesis 19:5

There has been much discussion about the meaning of the word 'know'. It may or may not be sexual. Even if it does have a sexual connotation it would be a demand for these men to be subjected to multiple violent homosexual rape. If this is the sin of Sodom it says absolutely nothing about the 'sinfulness' of consensual homosexual sex. Nobody would dream of using the social condemnation of heterosexual rape to say that heterosexuality is sinful.

But it is clear from the text that the sin of Sodom is not essentially sexual at all. Lot does **not** say in response to the townsmen: 'do not do this for it would be homosexual' or even: 'do not do this for it is a forbidden kind of sex'. What he actually says is: *Do nothing to these men for they have come under the shelter of my roof.* Genesis 19:8

Thus Lot appeals only to the requirements of hospitality. Strangers are to be treated as honoured guests, indeed as superiors. Remember that both he and Abraham had bowed low to them on their arrival. To abuse them for sexual pleasure would be to dishonour and humiliate them, to treat them as inferiors, which was anathema to the culture of the time. What is absolutely clear is that these Sodomite townsmen are intent on being extremely inhospitable towards the two strangers. The contrast with the fulsome hospitality offered by Abraham and by Lot could not be starker.

To try to protect his guests Lot offers the townsmen his two virgin daughters to use as they please: *Behold now, I have two daughters which have not known man; let me, I pray you, bring them out unto you, and do ye to them as is good in your eyes:* Genesis 19:8

This seems shockingly immoral to us but it is important for the story because it reveals the lengths to which Lot is prepared to go. Daughters were in those days subordinate to their father, effectively owned by him, part of his economic assets. If they are raped by the crowd, Lot will pay a high price because they will become unmarriageable, and he will be permanently responsible for their upkeep.

The true meaning of this gesture by Lot is therefore not an attempt to persuade the crowd to commit an acceptable heterosexual act instead of an abominable homosexual one, but rather a demonstration of the sacrifices he is willing to make to protect his guests.

Lot's reward

The story ends with the crowd of townsmen turning really nasty. They try to attack Lot, who of course is himself an outsider to Sodom. Lot is rescued by the two strangers who pull him back into the house in the nick of time. The townsmen go to break down the front door in an effort to reach Lot and his guests, but the strangers who are really angels instantly blind them: *And they smote the men that were at the door of the house with blindness, both small and great: so that they wearied themselves to find the door.* Genesis 19:11

The angels tell Lot to gather his family and help them to get out of the city of Sodom before it is destroyed under a hail of fire and brimstone. In this way Lot's reward parallels the reward given to Abraham. Both receive the promise of posterity whilst others are annihilated, Abraham in the form of a son and Lot by being allowed to escape.

This story has nothing to do with homosexuality

This is not a story about sex at all. Still less is it a story about the wickedness of same sex love. This is a story about reward and punishment. Contrary to what so many Christians claim, it is not a story about the virtue of heterosexuality and the vice of homosexuality. It is about the virtue of Abraham's and Lot's kind hospitality and the vice of the Sodomite townsmen's brutal inhospitality. The former is rewarded, the latter is punished. It would make no sense to say that Abraham and Lot are rewarded for being hospitable but the Sodomite townsmen are punished for being homosexual. It would undermine the whole point of the story. And yet this is what most mainstream Christian churches have taught. Abraham's future son and Lot's safe passage ensure their continuity and future, as Sodom and Gomorrah disappear under fire and brimstone, because they showed great hospitality to strangers. The two cities of Sodom and Gomorrah are completely destroyed, without hope of posterity, because of their flagrant inhospitality.

Many other subsequent passages in the Bible refer to the story of Sodom and Gomorrah, treating the Sodomites' sin purely as an outrage against the expected norms of hospitable behaviour towards strangers. For example, in Ezekiel we read: *This was the guilt of your sister, Sodom: she and her daughters had pride, surfeit of food and prosperous ease but did not aid the poor and needy.* Ezekiel 16:48-49

In the book of Wisdom the reference to Sodom's sin is 'bitter hatred of strangers' and 'making slaves of guests who were benefactors'. Other references occur in Isaiah, Jeremiah, and Zephaniah, where words such as oppression, injustice, partiality, lies and encouraging evil-doers appear.

Indeed Jesus himself confirms this in the Gospel of Matthew when he sends his disciples out to save 'the lost sheep of the House of Israel': *And whosoever shall not receive you, nor hear your words, when ye depart out of that house or city, shake off the dust of your feet. Verily I say unto you, it shall be more tolerable for the land of Sodom and Gomorrah in the day of judgement, than for that city.* Matthew 10:14-15

Jesus clearly has in mind here the offensively inhospitable actions of the Sodomite townsmen. What he is effectively saying is that those sodomites were punished for failing to respond to the expected norm of caring for the stranger in your midst, or in terms of his own teaching, the requirement to love your neighbour. If any of the people in the towns which the disciples are about to visit behave in this sodomite fashion, they will suffer the same judgement, but it will be worse because they are not just failing in their duty to 'love thy neighbour' they are in effect rejecting the Kingdom of God. Again it would make absolutely no sense for Jesus to say that if people reject the disciples they will suffer a worse penalty than that due to homosexuals.

The immorality of the 'traditional' interpretation

Just think for a moment about what the implications of the 'traditional' anti-gay interpretation peddled by the patriarchal churches actually are.

(1) As pointed out above, there can be no doubt that if the word 'know' means 'have sex with' then this sex is intended to be violent and non-consensual. It is rape. If the objects of this sexual attack were women it would still be rape. But nobody would then therefore say that any consensual male-female sex was wrong and due for punishment by God. It is a case of hypocritical double standards to say that disapproval of male rape means that any consensual male-male sex is wrong and due for punishment by God. It is also illogical.

(2) Are we really expected to believe that Lot's offering of his daughters to be raped by the crowd is a good moral example to be followed? There is no hint of criticism of Lot for doing this, either from the angels, or the Lord or the author of Genesis. These are not morals that can guide Christian lives today.

(3) God's destruction of Sodom and Gomorrah is cruel and arbitrary. If, as the patriarchal churches say, it is destroyed because of male homosexuality, why are they not appalled at the atrocity of killing innocent women and children who by definition cannot be guilty of what they call 'sodomy'?

Again, these are not morals that can guide Christian lives today.

(4) Similarly, remember God's promise to Abraham that if there were just ten righteous men then Sodom would be saved. Presumably we have to imagine that God thought there were not ten righteous men in Sodom. But if the sin that makes them unrighteous is homosexuality, and there are not even ten of them who are heterosexual, how on earth did the town continue to exist? Clearly there must have been some heterosexuals amongst them to keep the population going, and ten would not be enough! So if the churches are right. God must have broken his promise, and this is very immoral indeed. In fact the churches are wrong of course. God destroys Sodom for its inhospitality and it is perfectly possible for the population to continue even if 100% of the men fail to show respect for the norms of hospitality. But the churches in effect teach that God broke his promise to Abraham. Once more these are not morals that can guide Christian lives today.

(5) After his escape from Sodom, Lot has sex with his own daughters. They seduce him: *Come, let us make our father drink wine, and we will lie with him, that we may preserve seed of our father.* Genesis 20:32. This is a clear case of incest, and yet once again there is not the slightest suggestion anywhere in the text that this might be wrong or abhorrent. These really are not morals that can guide Christian lives today.

Thus, even if the patriarchal churches were correct in their interpretation of the story, which they are not, that interpretation simply cannot be used as a guide to moral conduct. It is outrageously immoral. And as we shall see later in the chapter on textual abuse they simply turn a blind eye to this fact. They also turn a blind eye to the fact that their so-called 'traditional' interpretation of the story is no such thing but dates actually only from the twelfth century.

The one lesson we can learn is the lesson it was actually intended to teach: show honour and respect to strangers. This of course was very important in the deserts of the Middle East three thousand years ago. If everywhere had been like Sodom it is doubtful that humanity would have survived. Honour and respect for strangers is of course also, as already noted, the precursor to Jesus' 'love commandments'.

A parallel story

In the Book of Judges there is story which sounds very similar. A Levite is on the road with his servant and his concubine. Night is drawing in and they look for shelter. They arrive at Gibeah and wait in the town centre to be offered hospitality. Nobody from the town offers them anything. And then a foreigner who, like Lot, happens to be temporarily resident takes them in. Just as they are all settling down for the night the townsmen come and demand to 'know' the Levite visitor. Like Lot the host offers them his virgin daughter, but the townsmen reject her. Then the Levite gives them his concubine: *and they knew her, and abused her all the night until the morning.* Judges 19:25

At dawn she is found dead in front of the house. Vengeance in this case is delivered by all the tribes of Israel who raze the town of Gibeah to the ground. Here the punishment is for a vicious heterosexual rape of atrocious savagery. The offence of the Gibean townsmen has nothing to do with homosexuality or heterosexuality. Just like the sin of the Sodomites, they indulged in gross inhospitality, and for it they were robbed of any hope of posterity. The lesson is the same and is crystal clear.

The sodomite behaviour of some Christian churches

It is a cruel irony that the whole language of sodomy and

sodomites has been applied to gay men. For two thousand years the Christian church has been responsible for persecuting, torturing and murdering gay people. You could say that the Christian churches have subjected LGBT people to extreme acts of inhospitality. Because of what, if we are being charitable, we could say is a misreading of the crime of Sodom and Gomorrah, the patriarchal Christian churches themselves perpetuate the true crime of Sodom and Gomorrah every day. Because of their policies of exclusion, condemnation and denial of basic human rights, it is arguably the churches which are sodomite rather than the LGBT people they victimise.

What the churches tend to do is to start with a predetermined prejudice against homosexuals and to then seek biblical justification for their exclusionary practices. A close reading of the Biblical texts concerning this story makes absolutely clear that there is no such justification here. We shall encounter this same situation with other texts used to attack gay people in the following chapters.

Many outspoken Christian leaders have in recent years called on gay people to 'repent and change'. Actually on the evidence presented here it is really these Christian leaders who need to 'repent and change' and apologise for their churches' uncharitable and unchristian behaviour towards LGBT people as God's children. The particular misuse of the story of Sodom and Gomorrah to demonise gay people, and to promote bigotry and homophobia, is an especially disgraceful example of the more general misuse of the Bible, which will be discussed later in chapter D7. It is especially disgraceful because Biblical scholars have known for a long time that the 'homosexual' interpretation of the story was wrong. To their credit, some churches have recognised this fact and no longer refer to it. Others, however, wilfully and culpably persist. Rather than LGBT people it is they who richly deserve the anathema carried by the word 'sodomite'.

LGBT Self-defence
Summary Sheet D1: The Story of Sodom

1. The key point here is Abraham's generous hospitality towards three strangers who arrive unexpectedly.

2. Abraham is told his hospitality will be rewarded with a son through whom his succession and blood-line will be guaranteed.

3. Lot replicates Abraham's hospitality towards the two strangers arriving in Sodom.

4. The townsmen of Sodom demand to 'know' the two strangers.

5. Lot resists their demand but refers only to the importance of hospitality.

6. Lot offers his virgin daughters to the townsmen to show how far he will go to fulfil the expectations of hospitality towards strangers.

7. Lot's reward will be to have his life and future guaranteed by escaping from Sodom's imminent destruction.

8. Many other Old Testament references to Sodom and a statement by Jesus himself confirm that this story is about the requirement to offer hospitality to strangers which might be said to foreshadow Jesus' commandment to love your neighbour.

9. The 'traditional' anti-gay version of this story is not traditional but dates from the twelfth century and is in fact highly immoral.

10. The patriarchal churches' inhospitality toward LGBT people arguably makes them guilty of the sin of Sodom and themselves 'sodomites'.

The Defensive Testament Chapter D2

Leviticus and the abominations

What exactly is an abomination?

Like 'Sodomite', abomination is another biblical word frequently used to condemn LGBT people. And also like 'Sodomite' many people use the word 'abomination' without really understanding what it means. They often think it is a sort of curse but actually it is nothing of the sort.

The word comes from the Book of Leviticus in the Old Testament. The specific 'abomination' reference usually used to attack LGBT people is: *With a male you shall not lie the lyings of a woman: it is an abomination.* Leviticus 18:22

This does seem to be a clear condemnation. Unlike the Genesis texts considered in chapter 1, here there is no 'story' from which we are expected to extract a moral lesson. Here we have an apparently unambiguous legal statement. However, it is in fact very far from being the condemnation of homosexuality which the mainstream churches claim.

Leviticus might as well have been called the Book of Abominations, because its speciality lies in making lists of them. The Hebrew word used is 'toevah' and the author of Leviticus regards an awful lot of things as 'toevah'. For example eating rabbits, pigs or shellfish, taking the silver or gold of idols, and the wearing of trousers by a woman are all 'toevah' or abominations.

In modern English the word 'abomination' sounds terrible. In essence, however, it denotes something which supposedly displeases God, and displeases Him for a particular reason. The ancient Israelites held an idealised worldview and believed all creation was intended by God to follow strict rules of uniformity and purity. Anything which appeared not to comply with the requirement for uniformity was regarded as an 'abomination'. The ritual purity laws of the Holiness code in Leviticus are designed to separate off 'God's chosen people', the Jews, from their Gentile neighbours, whom they supposed God did not choose or approve of.

For instance, having noticed that most fish had fins and scales, the ancient Israelites concluded that all fish should have both fins and scales. Prawns and shrimps do not fit this idealized view of fish. And because of this they are an aberration to be abominated. So the next time you see a religious person tucking into a prawn cocktail you should shriek loudly at them: 'you are an abomination!'

Similarly, land-based animals should possess cleft hooves and chew their cud. Pigs do not comply with this idealised view and so are another abomination. So no breakfast eggs and bacon in ancient Israel.

And when it comes to sex, idealised males should penetrate and idealised females should be penetrated. Male-male penetrative sex is a violation of this rule and is therefore an abomination. This strict idealisation of functions explains why there is no condemnation in Leviticus of female-female sex, or indeed of any other kind of male-male sex. The prohibition has nothing to do with sex and everything to do with the violation of boundaries.

The punishment for committing abominations
In many cases the punishment prescribed for committing abominations is death. This is so for *'lying with mankind as with womankind'*: *If a man lies with a male as with a woman, both of them shall be put to death for their abominable deed; they have forfeited their lives.* Leviticus 20:13

Other abominators to be put to death, according to the books of the Old Testament, include those who refuse to obey their parents, those who curse their parents and those who work on the Sabbath. Consider for example the fate of the disobedient son: *If a man have a stubborn and rebellious son, which will not obey the voice of his father, or the voice of his mother, and that when they have chastened him, will not hearken unto them: then shall his mother and his father lay hold on him, and bring him out unto the elders of his city, and unto the gate of his place; ....and all the men of the city shall stone him with stones, that he die.* Deuteronomy 22:18-21

Idealised sons are expected to obey their fathers. If they do not they are literally no longer sons, and so lose their place in the family and in society, and with it their right to live. They have become aberrant and abhorrent. They must be annihilated. This is how the death penalty operated in Ancient Israel.

The meaning of heterosexual sex in Ancient Israel

Ancient Israel was a thoroughly patriarchal society in which females were essentially regarded as property. Fathers owned their daughters until they were given in marriage to become wives owned by their husbands. This system of male domination, which was believed to be divinely ordained, is evident for example in the famous ten commandments given to Moses by God: *Thou shalt not covet thy neighbour's house, thou shalt not covet thy neighbour's wife, nor his manservant, nor his maidservant, nor his ox, nor his ass, nor anything that is thy neighbour's.* Exodus 20:17

It is indicative of the lowly status of women in Ancient Israel that in the list of belongings a man's wife comes after his house. Sexual acts reflected this institutionalised gross inequality. Men symbolised their ownership of females by penetrating them. And thus in this context adulterous sex meant infringing property rights rather than simply breaching moral codes. So in this culture if a man has sex with a married woman he has not so much broken his own marriage vows to his wife or offended against a moral law, as violated the property rights of another man, the married woman's husband. The adulterous married woman also violates the property rights of her husband because she is behaving as if she were not his property.

A woman is expected to remain a virgin until she is married. If she is discovered not to be a virgin, the punishment is death. After marriage she is forbidden to have sex with anyone except her husband. If she does, the punishment is death. There is, however, no expectation that a man will remain a virgin until he is married. And so long as he avoids trampling on another man's property rights he can have sex with women without fear of repercussions.

The meaning of 'lyings of a woman' in Ancient Israel

What the ancient Israelite male cannot do though is *'lie with a man as with a woman'* without running the risk of being executed. But what exactly are *'the lyings of a woman'*?

Clearly there must be more to it than simply lying down. We are not talking here about just being in the same bed or on the same couch. There must be some sort of erotic activity going on. But what?

At what point does the offence of doing *'the lyings of a woman'* actually occur? Does it matter if they just touch? Caressing? Hugging? What about kissing? Kissing different parts of the body, on the lips, the genitals? Suppose they engage in mutual masturbation: would that constitute an offence, an abomination?

No. The Old Testament never refers to any of these and appears utterly unconcerned about such activities. They are never mentioned. What the author of Leviticus is exclusively concerned with is anal penetration. In the previous chapter we saw how the word *'lie'* was used to describe what Lot's daughters did with their father. These were acts of vaginal penetration and so we can be confident that the focus here is exclusively on sexual penetration.

Further confirmation comes in the very next verse of

Leviticus: *You shall not lie with any animal so as to defile yourself by it: and a woman shall not stand in front of an animal so that it lies down: that is confusion.* Leviticus 18:23

This is clearly a prohibition on males penetrating animals and females being penetrated by animals.

Thus the 'abomination' being anathematised in *'the lyings of a woman'* is not homosexuality as such but only the very specific act of one man penetrating the anus of another man.

This text has nothing to do with homosexuality

This proscription of anal intercourse between men has absolutely nothing to do with same sex love. As discussed above, penetrative sex in the culture of Ancient Israel is all about domination and possession of females by males. What the male author of Leviticus is so anxious about is not the act of anal inter-course itself but rather what it means for Ancient Israelite society. And what it means for that society is men acting as if they were women. He sees this as a terrible confusion of categories and a grave challenge to God's divine ordering in which males do the dominating, possessing and penetrating. It is therefore a huge threat to the social fabric and to the patriarchal privileges which that social fabric affords to males. As St Augustine would write later in the fourth century, *The body of a man is as superior to that of a woman as the soul is to the body.* Quoted in Helmaniak (2000) p.46

In the terms of Leviticus, men who allow themselves to be penetrated, dominated and possessed are not behaving as 'homosexuals' (a concept or category completely unknown in Ancient Israel) but rather as women. And for men to behave as women is to undermine the very basis of the sexual hierarchy on which the stability and functioning of the whole society depends. The only way to deal with this threat is to kill it. Just like the disobedient son, men who penetrate each other have ceased to be the category of person they are supposed to be, and which justifies their place in society. And with no defined place in society they lose their right to live. Their continued existence is not to be tolerated.

The irrelevance of Leviticus 18:22 now

In actual fact the use of Leviticus 18:22 to condemn gay sex is highly problematic for homophobic religious leaders because the text by implication actually permits same-sex erotic activity, so long as no penetration takes place. Only if one male penetrates another does the activity turn into the crime of 'males acting as females', and only then does it come under the scope of this law. Furthermore, what this law is designed to protect is not hetero-sexuality but a supposedly divinely ordained sexual hierarchy which privileges males and treats women as virtually subhuman; something that we now would regard as totally unacceptable, completely immoral and definitely unchristian.

The Book of Leviticus was written approximately 3500 years ago in the Bronze Age. It addresses the needs of a prehistoric society in the Middle East whose survival was constantly under threat. That social and cultural context is so remote from us and alien to us that it is really quite ludicrous to assume that its condemnations can simply be taken literally, as some Christian fundamentalists do. Many of the rules relate to the need to promote childbirth and population growth, the very reverse of what we need today. Others seek to distinguish Jews from surrounding hostile Gentile nations, and yet others are based on principles of hygiene, even if couched in religious language. It was of course not a good idea to eat shellfish in the desert then. Today we have fridges.

Nobody takes all the rules of Leviticus literally today. Even extreme Christian fundamentalists do not kill their children for disobedience. And yet they feel able to cite Leviticus 18:22 to attack LGBT people who they do not like. They quote the proscriptions of Leviticus in a highly selective way that supports a predetermined prejudice. They do not, for example, waste their time ranting about people wearing mixed fabrics (condemned in Leviticus 19:19) or men having sex with a menstruating woman (condemned in Leviticus 18:19) or even incest (condemned in Leviticus 18:6) but rather focus on 18:22 in the mistaken belief that it condemns homosexuality, rather than anathematising the infringement of hierarchical boundaries and category confusions which are its real target.

On what rational basis can some prohibitions be regarded as still in force and others as dispensable? If you believe that the Bible is God's inerrant word for all time how can you possibly pick and choose? Logically of course you cannot. However the recourse to Leviticus 18:22 to deny LGBT people equal rights is not based on logic.

What LGBT people need to do is to say that until Christian fundamentalists boycott shellfish restaurants, stop wearing polycotton shirts, and stone to death their wayward offspring, there is no obligation to listen to their diatribes about homosexuality being an abomination.

The importance of repetition

Biblical scholars generally think you should pay more heed if condemnations are repeated many times. The condemnation of adultery, for example, is repeated time and time again (Leviticus, Exodus, Numbers and Deuteronomy in the Old Testament and in many passages of the New Testament, including statements by Jesus himself). By contrast the *only* mention of male-male sexual relations in the whole of the Old Testament is in these two short verses of Leviticus.

If it is true that God views men having sex with men as completely unacceptable and abominable, and deserving of death, surely the condemnations would be repeated again and again as they are for adultery. Why aren't they? Moreover, if it is true that God views homosexuality per se as completely unacceptable and abominable, why is there not a single mention of female-female sexual relations anywhere in the Old Testament?

The answer to these questions is self-evident. There is no condemnation of homosexuality to be found in the Old Testament. The writers of its constituent books are not at all concerned about homosexuality. They are only interested in giving divine sanction to the patriarchal structure of their society and ruthlessly punishing anybody who breaches the tight boundaries of inequality between the sexes.

Thus scriptural support for homophobia in Leviticus is not just weak; it is totally absent.

The relevance of the Old Testament

A further problem for anti-gay Christians trying to use Leviticus to prop up their denunciation of LGBT identities and relationships is that Jesus seems to have said that he came to put an end to its laws. As far as he was concerned there were only two commandments: *Thou shalt love the Lord thy God with all thy heart, and with all thy soul, and with all thy mind…..Thou shalt love thy neighbour as thyself. On those two commandments hang all the law and the prophets.* Matthew 24:36-40

The legalistic codification of the rules in the Law and the Prophets of the Old Testament had been superceded by the inbreaking of the Kingdom of God through the arrival of His Son, the Messiah. Everything from then onwards was to be judged against the simple criterion of whether it promotes the love of God and the love of one's neighbour. As St Paul put it: *You are not under law but under grace.* Romans 6:14

Paul sees that the strict rules of the Old Testament were appropriate for a particular stage in the gradual revelation of God to His people but they were not meant to be binding laws on everybody for all time. Jesus, for example, points out that Moses permitted divorce because of the weakness of the people but that this was not how it would always be (Matthew 19:8). Paul also believes that living by rules for their own sake is an impoverishment and a diminishment of what human beings should aspire to. The new covenant inaugurated by Jesus is: *not of the letter, but of the spirit: for the letter killeth, but the spirit giveth life.* 2 Corinthians 3:6

The laws of the Old Testament are all about defining what is ideal, what is pure, allegedly, in God's eyes. This results in a very strange picture of a supposedly loving heavenly Father who only wants to see healthy adult, able bodied, affluent heterosexual Jewish men, and is happy for children, women, homosexuals, the sick, the poor, the elderly, the lepers, the blind, the illegitimate, the deaf, the mute, the demon possessed, the mentally ill, and everybody who is not Jewish to be excluded from his sight, by imposing restrictions, by casting out from society, or by murder through execution. This whole system of purity laws purported to keep the Jews as a 'holy' nation separate, different and distinct from all the other 'unclean' Gentile nations.

Jesus' coming overthrew the idea that only those socially defined as 'normal' are loved by God. He dramatically demonstrated this by deliberately choosing his friends from amongst those inhabiting the excluded 'unclean' spaces outside the Jewish purity laws. And as Jeffrey John (2001) has pointed out in his study of the meaning to be found in the New Testament miracles, Jesus systematically undid all the prohibitions of Leviticus by blessing, curing and affirming people in all the groups which it had marginalised. And of course Jesus' coming also overthrew the idea that God only loved Jews.

The implications of this 'overthrowing' are far reaching. At the very least it means that even if there were a condemnation of homosexuality in the Old Testament, which as we have seen there is not, its relevance and applicability would now have to be considered against Jesus' love commandments. With this in mind William Countryman (1988) has argued that this means that for genuine Christians 'only intent to harm renders a sexual act impure' (op cit p.86). Since by definition same sex love cannot at the same time be an intention to harm, it cannot be considered impure.

For many Christian fundamentalists this is a hard concept to grasp. In practice it means accepting that Jesus would be on the side of LGBT people in a gay pride march rather than on the fundamentalists' side as they wave their banners quoting Leviticus, for example. And that is because it is the gay marchers rather than the Christian protesters who are seeking to fulfil Christ's commandment to love your neighbour.

If we take Christ's words seriously, we have to conclude that any interpretation of biblical texts which damages people or hurts them cannot be the right interpretation. To claim that any such interpretation is 'traditional' will not do. If it offends against the twin Christian principles of love of God and love of neighbour it must be wrong. So called 'traditional' teachings change over time and the churches acknowledge that many have been wrong before. 'Traditional' teachings on slavery and witch-craft, for example, are now denounced. If any Christian church wants to carry on persecuting LGBT people and remain true to Christ, it is incumbent on it to show how such actions can possibly be considered loving. Can the church prove that mutual, caring, loving same sex relationships are damaging to the partners sharing them? Are there really good reasons to deny gay people the love and intimacy enjoyed by straight people? Is it really healthy for young gay Christians to learn to hate themselves and pray desperately that God will make them into something totally different? Is the current situation in which loyal church members are expected to endure loneliness, isolation, frustration, self-hatred, rejection, violence, mental illness, despair and suicide really an expression of the church's love for its gay neighbours? These questions hardly need answering.

Is the Church an abomination?

According to the Old Testament definitions which we have discussed, an abomination occurs when someone or something stops being the thing it is ideally supposed to be. The son should be obedient, the wife should be faithful, the male should be a penetrator of females.

And what about the Christian churches? What are they supposed to be? They are supposed to proclaim the love of God and spread the good news of Jesus Christ 'to all the earth'. When they fail to do this, and instead begin to do the very reverse of what Jesus actually taught, it is arguable that they themselves are on the road to becoming an abomination. By promoting homophobia and prejudice against LGBT people on the basis of 'scriptural support', which is in fact no such thing, they ally themselves with the worst elements of Old Testament thinking and betray their calling to preach Christ crucified. Here is the ecclesiastical equivalent of the disobedient son and the unfaithful wife, abominations deserving of annihilation.

Just as the churches who labelled gay men 'sodomites' are ipso facto in themselves behaving in a sodomite, i.e. inhospitable, fashion, so the churches who label LGBT people an abomination, are ipso facto themselves acting in an abominable, i.e. disordered, manner. Leviticus tells us that abominations are abhorrent in the sight of God. The conduct of some churches towards LGBT people does not just affront any principle of fairness, justice and equality. It is a thoroughgoing abomination in this sense. One can only imagine that it is a gross affront to the loving God who has created us all in His likeness.

LGBT Self defence
Summary Sheet D2: Leviticus and the abominations

1. An abomination is someone or something which does not comply with the Jewish purity laws set out in the Book of Leviticus and other books of the Old Testament. These laws were believed to describe what was acceptable and unacceptable to God, but were actually intended to separate Jews from their Gentile neighbours.

2. Things which offend the purity laws include eating shellfish, wearing mixed fabrics, and having sex with a menstruating woman.

3. Ancient Israel was a strongly patriarchal society in which women were treated as inferior and in effect the property first of their father and then of their husband.

4. The abomination of 'lying with mankind as with womankind' is not a condemnation of homosexuality per se. It has nothing to do with sex. It is a revulsion at the idea of a male acting as a female. This is perceived as a threat to the system of male domination and the penalty is death.

5. The abomination thus relates only to anal penetration. There is no condemnation here of any other type of gay sexual activity which does not amount to 'lying as with a woman'. Nor is there any condemnation of female-female sexual activity.

6. There is no other reference to male or female homosexuality in the whole of the Old Testament.

7. Biblical scholars believe that condemnations of particular acts carry more weight if they are repeated many times and are less significant if they are not repeated.

8. Leviticus was written 3500 years ago for a Bronze Age society in the desert. Its culture is alien and its laws cannot

simply be applied to us now. We would now regard its treatment of women as deeply shocking, immoral and unchristian.

9. Christian fundamentalists make selective use of the Old Testament prohibitions and proscriptions, yet there is no logical justification for enforcing some and ignoring others. Their selection is based on a pre-existing prejudice against gay people. They do not, for example, stone to death their disobedient children.

10. Anti-gay Christians have to justify their use of Old Testament texts in the light of both St Paul and Jesus himself declaring that its rules and laws had been superceded. All laws need to be justified against the twin commandments of love of God and love of neighbour.

11. Churches which continue to condemn LGBT people must therefore demonstrate that their denial of equal rights to LGBT people, with all the negative consequences for their quality of life which then ensue, is a more loving act than affirming gay relationships would be.

12. Churches which use Leviticus to attack gay rights are arguably also themselves an abomination in the sense that they have ceased to be the thing they are supposed to be: preachers of the good news of Jesus Christ to all God's children.

The Defensive Testament Chapter D3

The So-Called 'Creation Ordinances'

Compulsory heterosexual marriage

Over the past five hundred years, almost all the Christian churches have come to regard the institution of monogamous heterosexual marriage as compulsory because it is ordained directly by God. Although the driving force behind this development was the emergence of Protestantism in the sixteenth century, this idea that everybody is naturally heterosexual and called either to total abstinence in celibacy, or to totally monogamous commitment in the 'holy estate of marriage', is now the official dogma of catholic, orthodox, and virtually every other mainstream brand of Christianity. Previously the Catholic Church and others had viewed the single celibate state as superior to the marital state.

Consequent upon this development has been the inevitable conclusion that LGBT people are a 'threat' to marriage and the family. It is normal and normative to marry a person of the opposite sex. Wanting to have any kind of relationship with a person of the same sex is thus necessarily abnormal and deviant. All that is on offer to a self-accepting Christian lesbian or a gay man who wants to be loyal to church teaching is lifelong abstinence. Anything else ipso facto is viewed as contrary to God's creation ordinances. In the face of such ecclesiastical totalitarianism, backed in most 'Christian' countries by the force of law and the threat of imprisonment or worse, millions of LGBT people over the centuries have been faced with a stark choice: live in lonely isolation or contract unhappy and unfulfilling marriages.

The so-called 'creation ordinances'

Marriage is one of three so-called 'creation ordinances'. The concept of a 'creation ordinance' is associated mainly with protestant evangelicals who believe that at the beginning of creation God instituted a set of inviolable laws, some governing nature (such as the law of gravity), and others governing human conduct. These ordinances are taken to be built into a presumed 'covenant' between God and man designed to keep the created world secure and orderly. Evangelicals appeal to the first two chapters of the Book of Genesis to justify these claims. They have to acknowledge though that the 'covenant' is presumed because it is in fact nowhere mentioned in Genesis. The ordinances governing human conduct are: (1) keeping the Sabbath (2) labour (to work to subdue the earth for the glory of God) and (3) marriage.

It is important for LGBT people to understand the force of the argument being deployed here. The claim is that these 'creation ordinances' are God's plan. They are therefore not simply human inventions which can be changed. They are not up for discussion. To be against them is to be against God. Any society which ignores the law of gravity will come to grief. Evangelical Christians believe the same about God's laws governing marriage. And as has been shown in the vitriolic attacks on gay rights in the USA, they are prepared to go to enormous lengths to uphold them. From an LGBT point of view this is an extremely dangerous idea.

It is also a very wrong idea. The main biblical texts quoted in support of the marriage ordinance are: *(1) So God created man in his own image, in the image of God created he him; male and female created he them. And God blessed them, and God said unto them, be fruitful, and multiply, and replenish the earth, and subdue it.* Genesis 1:27:28

And *(2) And the Lord God said, it is not good that the man should be alone; I will make him an help meet for him.* Genesis 2:18

And then God makes the first woman, Eve (Genesis 2:22), and tells Adam: *(3) Therefore shall a man leave his father and his mother, and shall cleave unto his wife: and they shall be one flesh.* Genesis 2:24

From these few isolated verses protestant evangelicals conclude that God endorses the institution of marriage and the modern western nuclear family with 2.4 children and a dog. More threateningly, they also conclude that God abhors everything else, polygamy, divorce, and especially homosexuality.

Problems with the ordinance of compulsory heterosexual marriage

What is bizarre about the evangelicals' persistent attachment to the idea that God is here in Genesis sanctifying their particular take on marriage and family life as inviolable, is their failure to recognise that the rest of the Bible does not at all conform to it. The Bible stories which follow on from Genesis offer a rich tapestry of diverse family structures and relationships between and within the sexes. We read, for example, of polygamy, serial monogamy, wife-swapping, concubines, male-male relationships, female-female relationships, rape, child abuse, incest and all manner of weird and wonderful sexual conduct, most of it simply taken for granted without a hint of condemnation from God. And of course the one thing we do not read about is the domestic nuclear bliss of hubby and the misses and their adorable two children and pets.

They also fail to recognise that the concept of 'one flesh' does not necessarily mean husband and wife copulating but rather implies the creation of a new kinship group, a new unit within society. This is the meaning of it 'not being good for man to be alone'. Humans are sociable beings and need to be involved in structures of relationships in order to thrive.

They seem unaware too that God has not created everybody male and female but has chosen to make a significant percentage of the human population intersexed.*This group is composed of individuals with a range of medical conditions but all members have one factor in common: that for each one, when all the usual determinants of maleness and femaleness are put together, that person cannot be clearly assigned to a male or female gender. Such conditions are more common than is generally perceived, affecting up to 2 percent of the population.* Hare (2007) p.98

Two percent of the population means that literally millions of human beings across the world were not created male and female and yet are still God's children. The existence of this group clearly shows up the absurdly simplistic nature of the evangelical assumption that there is a universal rigid distinction between male and female. The reality is that maleness and femaleness are on a continuum. We may be mostly male or mostly female but we are never exclusively one or the other.

The most bizarre thing of all, however, is that supporters of the marriage ordinance idea fail, quite astonishingly, to understand that the life and teaching of Jesus, the Son of the God who is supposed to have created the ordinance, do not conform to it at all.

Jesus' criticism of marriage

Jesus himself never married, formed close relationships with other men and some women in connection with which the word 'love' is repeatedly used in the Gospel accounts, and developed a very special relationship with one particular male disciple whom the Gospel of John describes as 'beloved'. This will be discussed in more depth in chapter A1 of the Affirmative Testament.

In his teaching Jesus was actually very critical of the institution of marriage.

On one occasion he is being interrogated by the Sadducees, a Jewish religious group who did not believe in life after death. They try to point out the absurdity of believing in a post-death resurrection by asking about marriage. Moses had commanded that if a man died and left a wife but no children then his brother must marry the wife and produce children for him. If this happened again and again you could get a situation in which when the wife finally died she might have been married to as many as say, seven brothers. Thinking they can make Jesus look ridiculous they ask: 'in the resurrection whose wife will she be?'

Jesus replies: *You fall into error because you do not know the scriptures nor do you know the power of God. For when they rise from the dead, they neither marry nor are given in marriage, but are like the angels in heaven.* Mark 12:24-27

For the Sadducees and for many, if not most, people in those days marriage was essentially about social position, property and inheritance. The whole point of Moses' law was to maintain the status quo. Marriage of the widow to the surviving eldest brother was the way to keep the power, standing and wealth of the dead brother within the family group.

Jesus, however, is absolutely not interested in maintaining the status quo. Quite the opposite. His answer makes clear that the so-called indissoluble institution of marriage will in fact be immediately dissolved in the Kingdom of God. This supposedly fundamental bedrock societal institution has no future under God's reign.

Furthermore, even in the present to be a follower of Jesus, and to be part of the Kingdom, it is necessary here and now to abandon all the paraphernalia of property, wealth and status. In Matthew chapter 19 he tells the rich young man who asks what he must do to inherit eternal life that he must sell everything he has and give the money to the poor. Jesus goes on to make the famous comment about it being *'easier for a camel to go through the eye of a needle than for a rich man to enter the Kingdom of Heaven.'* Rich here does not just mean having lots of money. It means giving up all the attachments to this world which hold you back from responding to and embracing the love of God.

Therefore, far from endorsing the repressive current Christian orthodoxy that God commands everyone to contract a marriage with a person of the opposite sex, Jesus views the institution of heterosexual marriage as an obstacle to be overcome. He is very critical indeed of its effects, going so far as to imply that husbands should leave their wives to be a true follower of his (as indeed the disciples did): *And everyone that hath forsaken houses, or brethren, or sisters, or father, or mother, **or wife**, or children, or lands, for my name's sake, shall receive an hundredfold, and shall inherit everlasting life.* Matthew 20:29

The patriarchal Christian churches persistently, and arguably wilfully, ignore how radical Jesus' teaching actually is. In the Gospel of Luke we read: *If any man come to me, and hate not his father, and mother, **and wife**, and children, and brethren, and sisters, yea, and his own life also, he cannot be my disciple.* Luke 15:26

Being a follower of Jesus means divesting yourself of everything that ties you to merely human social structures, including the institution of heterosexual marriage. The clear and unmistakable message is that these structures are ultimately transient and will pass away, and if your life, identity and relationships are locked into them you, too, will pass away unaware of the fullness of life with God and with no hope of resurrection.

The question of sexuality

It has been assumed by many people that Jesus meant sexuality would be abolished in the Kingdom of Heaven along with marriage. But he does not say this. All Jesus implies is that the whole institutional complex of rights and duties, ownership, and social standing designed to provide political and economic security and maintain structures of domination, which is what the institution of marriage is essentially about, will be got rid of. And, of course, he says that they should be done away with now, not only because they create distractions from our relationship with God but also because they are full of injustices and oppression.

33

Erotophobes may well be wrong to conclude that Jesus meant there would be no sex in heaven for the following reasons:

he specifically does not include people enjoying having sex in his reasons for criticising the institution of marriage;

he does not appear in any of the gospels to adopt a negative attitude towards sexual pleasure and eroticism (this comes into Christianity later with the churches' versions of St Paul);

he appears to take delight in all the joys of life and refers often to feasting and partying;

he is perfectly at ease with sexually active, marginalised people, e.g. the prostitute who washes his feet with her tears and who 'loved much' (Luke 7:36- 50);

resurrection is not resuscitation: the Christian belief is that God will provide new resurrection bodies which may well be capable of erotic delight.

Far more important than sexuality for Jesus is being implicated in social structures which jeopardise our entry to the Kingdom of God. In Luke's version of the Sadducees' story Jesus is reported as saying: *The sons of this age marry and are given in marriage; but those who are accounted worthy to attain to that age and to the resurrection from the dead neither marry nor are given in marriage, for they cannot die anymore, because they are equal to the angels and are sons of God being sons of the resurrection.* Luke 20:35-36

As Jennings (2003) notes, the two critical phrases in this passage are 'the sons of this age' and the 'sons of the resurrection'. These are clearly being treated as two entirely different things. 'Sons' obviously implies both sexes since the reference is to those who marry (men) and those who are given in marriage (women). Clearly it is unlikely that Jesus was thinking of same sex marriage at this point! A better modern translation would be 'children' rather than 'sons'.

What matters though is that there are these two groups of people. The people of the first group are locked into the temporary and passing life of 'this age'. The people of the second group, however, are already in some sense living the resurrection as children of God and followers of Jesus.

In this perspective then it is not so much being LGBT that is the 'threat' to gaining eternal life but rather the very institution of marriage itself, so loved and idolised by the patriarchal Christian churches, which poses the greatest threat to the hope of resurrection. How ironic this is! These self-same churches spend so much time and energy demonising and condemning gay people, and yet it is their own idolatry, worshipping the idol of heterosexist marriage, which the God they claim to represent actually tells us he regards as a bar to entry into heaven! When you read the biblical texts carefully it really is incomprehensible that these churches can continue to peddle such distortions of Jesus' message. The only possible explanation is that they feel the fear and hatred of homosexuality with such overwhelming and visceral intensity that it overrides their reason and understanding. Leaders of these churches would do well to remember their God's salutary condemnation of hypocrisy: *How canst thou say to thy brother, Brother, let me pull out the mote that is in thine eye, when thou thyself beholdest not the beam that is in thine own eye? Thou hypocrite, cast out first the beam out of thine own eye, and then shalt thou see clearly to pullout the mote that is in thy brother's eye.* Luke 6:42

They might also consider the condemnation in the same gospel of anyone who misleads the innocent: *it were better for him that a millstone were hanged about his neck and he were cast into the sea.* Luke 17:2

Divorce as a breach of loyalty

The patriarchal churches' buttressing of heterosexual monogamous marriage has often involved appealing to Jesus' comments on divorce. These too have been widely misinterpreted, misunderstood and used to mislead.

One of the most frequently cited texts comes in a discussion between Jesus and a group of Pharisees who were particularly legalistic Jews. They ask him whether it is lawful for a man to divorce his wife, as Moses had allowed. Jesus says that Moses only permitted this because of 'their hardness of heart'. Basically it was a concession to human weakness and fallibility but given by Moses, not by God.

But from the beginning of creation, 'God made them male and female. For this reason a man shall leave his father and mother and the two shall be one flesh so that they are no longer two but one.' What therefore God has yoked together let not humanity separate. And in the house again the disciples asked about this. And he said to them, 'whoever dismisses his woman and marries another commits adultery with her; and whoever dismisses her man and marries another she commits adultery'. Mark 10:1-12

The key point in this text is that Jesus does not refer to husbands and wives, but to males and females, men and women. He is not therefore actually addressing the (human) institution of marriage. He is talking about two people of opposite sex who naturally desire to be together and become 'one flesh'. He is suggesting that God smiles on such delightful relationships and, as it were, gives them his blessing. It is therefore not for any human institution, be it marriage, the family, the law or religion to interfere. So the teaching is essentially about personal loyalty and commitment, and certainly not about the supposed 'holy estate of matrimony'. There can here be no condemnation of 'living in sin' because there is here no legitimation of a marriage institution with which such 'sinfulness' can be contrasted.

It is also an interesting implication of Jesus' words that the natural sexual desires of the two people which drive them to want to be together are approved and designated as 'of God'. Here then is a further reason to suspect and hope that sex may be on the agenda in heaven.

What Jesus is principally concerned with is relationships grounded in mutual desire and based on a freely given loyalty. It is these which receive divine sanctification. And in the passage from the Gospel of Mark quoted above, it is clear that these relationships are characterised by equality between males and females. Both men and women commit 'adultery' if they dismiss their partner and begin a new relationship.

Moreover, Jesus seems to have in mind an analogy with a person's decision to become a disciple. As we have seen a would-be follower of Jesus is required to break away from his 'blood' kinship family of origin, leaving father, mother, brothers, and sisters in order to commit him/herself body and soul to the Kingdom of God. In the same way a man or woman has to leave the natural parental family to make a total commitment to a new permanent love relationship. In both cases any breach of loyalty to the new commitment is tantamount to 'adultery'. In one sense Jesus is simply stating the obvious. If you deceive and betray someone to whom you have given your life, you have caused a terrible rupture which is inescapably painful and damaging.

It is important to be clear about this teaching. Jesus is pointing to a truth which any of us can learn from experience for ourselves. This is not the same as telling people they must obey the law and will be horribly punished if they do not. Indeed in the one case of legalistic adultery brought to him, Jesus effectively repudiates the law as a mere human contrivance, and is extraordinarily compassionate. Once more it is those good old legal eagles of Judaism, the Pharisees, who do the finger wagging: *This woman was taken in adultery, in the very act. Now Moses in the law commanded us, that such should be stoned: but what sayest thou?* John 8: 6

Jesus says nothing for a long time. This is just a tragedy. But the Pharisees persist. Instead of focussing on the wickedness of the woman, Jesus turns the question round on to her accusers: *He that is without sin among you, let him cast the first stone.*

The Gospel of John then tells us that *'being convicted by their own conscience'* they then leave the scene one by one. Jesus thus shows them and us that this is not a matter of rules and laws but rather a question of simple eternal truth. We should not judge lest we be judged also and then inevitably also found wanting. We humans are not in a fit state to make harsh laws and impose savage punishments. God alone is able to judge. No man is left to condemn the woman. Jesus assures her that he does not condemn her either. He tells her to go and sin no more. Not sinning any more does not mean 'obey the rules in future', as so many modern day self-righteous Pharisees want to say, but rather strive always to do what is good and right and will not cause future harm and hurt to self or neighbour.

Procreation and same sex relationships

Contrary to the impression created by the patriarchal Christian churches, gospel teaching on marriage is therefore remarkably affirming of erotic enjoyment, carnal desire and sexual pleasure. Unions arising out of reciprocated sexual attraction are seen as delighting God. What does not delight God, according to Jesus, is tying such relationships up in institutional complexities, whose only aim is to preserve social and economic advantage in this world. To do this is effectively to resist the dominion of the Kingdom of God. The guiding principle in sexuality is the same as in all areas of human experience: the love of God and the love of neighbour.

There does not seem prima facie any evidence here for the condemnation of same sex loving relationships. In fact, before the advent of same sex marriage and civil partnerships, it could be argued that homosexual liaisons were privileged in the eyes of God in the sense that they represent a form of pure love unsullied and uncontaminated by involvement in patriarchal systems of domination, characterised by subordination (and often ownership) of women, and concern with the transmission of wealth and property through the generations.

Indeed, the very fact that homosexual couples cannot by themselves reproduce does seem to be a positive factor in the ideal picture of conjugal relationships before our eyes in the gospel texts. Once children arrive a family structure is perforce in place. Then the danger is that time, energy and resources will be directed away from love of God and love of neighbour towards planning in this world for advancement, security and inheritance.

Of course the very reverse argument has been used by Christian leaders and spokespersons. They say marriage exists for the procreation of children and, since gay couples cannot reproduce, they cannot marry either. Historically this view has been linked with a great distaste for the body and all things carnal, and has led to a real fear of eroticism and sexuality in general. Only married husbands and wives are allowed to have sex and then only if they intend to allow children to be born. This teaching was given a further nasty twist, first by St Augustine, who said that the disgusting lust necessary for sexual intercourse was the channel through which original sin is transmitted from one generation to the next, and then again later by St Thomas Aquinas who concluded that any sexual act at all which is not directed towards procreation is inherently sinful. Sex outside marriage, adultery, homosexuality and masturbation are therefore all to be condemned without reservation. This is still the teaching of the Catholic Church, and many others, in the twenty-first century.

At this point a rather unlikely hero comes to our rescue. In his first letter to the Corinthians St Paul, whose supposedly anti-gay teachings will be discussed in the next two chapters, elaborates Jesus' view of conjugal relationships in a way that emphasises the importance of sex in bonding couples together: *The husband should give to his wife her conjugal rights, and likewise the wife to her husband.* 1 Corinthians 7:3

Defraud ye not one the other, except it be with consent for a time, that ye may give yourselves to fasting and prayer; and come together again, that Satan tempt you not for your incontinency. 1 Corinthians 7:5

Here there is no reference to having sex in order to beget offspring. It is all about satisfying your partner, and doing so on the basis of equality with a wife who has the same expectation of sexual satisfaction. And if the couple are going to refrain from sex, then this too should be on the basis of consent between the two of them. As with the gospel passages discussed above, we are here dealing with a view of marriage based on mutual sexual attraction. Paul also works out the implications of becoming 'one flesh': *'For the wife does not have authority over her own body, but the husband does; likewise the husband does not have authority over his own body, but the wife does.* 1 Corinthians 7:3-4

In a committed relationship, you give your body to your partner completely and this is supposed to work both ways in full equality. Paul even sees the siring of children in a negative light, to the extent that having children distracts Christians from doing the work of the Lord, which should be their first and foremost preoccupation.

Here we have a picture of loving relationships with which LGBT people can fully identify. There is nothing in this picture to exclude LGBT relationships. Same sex pairings are just as capable as cross-sex pairings of living out their sexual desires within the context of mutual pleasure, care and enduring loyalty.

The real 'Creation Ordinance'

The real creation ordinance implicit in the Genesis texts, then, is not a ferocious set of rules to oppress women and exclude whole categories of people. Rather, it is the two commandments given by Jesus to love God and love your neighbour. And if you enter into an exclusive relationship with a beloved partner, then you should do so on the basis of equality, trust and commitment. Enjoy 'not being alone' and bring pleasure and satisfaction to each other. Remain loyal. Thrive and flourish in the mutual care and support which your being 'one flesh' brings.

LGBT Self defence
Summary Sheet D3: The So-Called 'Creation Ordinances'

1. The idea of compulsory heterosexual marriage for everybody only emerged during the Protestant reformation of the 16th century. Before that the Catholic Church and others had viewed the single celibate state as superior.

2. This idea is now linked with the so-called 'creation ordinances': elements of a presumed covenant (not specifically stated in Genesis) between God and mankind in the Garden of Eden before the Fall. These are regarded as inviolable laws built in to nature by God just like the law of gravity.

3. The 'ordinances' are: (1) Keeping the Sabbath (2) Labour (3) Marriage

4. The marriage ordinance relies on Genesis texts about being made in God's image, making them male and female, the two becoming one flesh and being 'fruitful'.

5. Protestant evangelicals assume the Genesis texts endorse the modern western form of marriage and nuclear family but the Bible stories following Genesis do not at all conform to this pattern.

6. Jesus' life does not conform to the marriage ordinance, or the other two.

7. Jesus' teaching is very critical of the institution of marriage. He is clear that there will be no marriage in heaven.

8. Jesus condemns the institution of marriage as a means of preserving power, status and wealth in this world.

9. To be a follower of his, Jesus says it is necessary to forsake family and spouses, even to hate them for the sake of the Kingdom of God.

10. There is no condemnation of sexual desire and enjoyment in

the gospels.

11. Jesus emphasises the 'chosen' family of likeminded people committed to discipleship over the 'given' family of blood ties. This makes the 'normal' family the 'threat' to Christian values. LGBT families are more like the groupings Jesus advocates.

12. Jesus does not take a legalistic view of divorce but sees it as a tragic breach of loyalty.

13. The gospels and St Paul picture marriage as a relationship of mutual love, support and bodily service. There is nothing in this picture to exclude LGBT people.

The Defensive Testament Chapter D4

St Paul and Living 'Beyond Nature'

Romans 1: the number one 'terror text'

Probably the most frequently cited Biblical text used to condemn LGBT people comes in chapter one of St Paul's letter to the Romans: *They exchanged the truth of God for a lie and revered and worshipped the creature rather than the creator, who is blessed forever. Amen. Therefore, God handed them over to degrading passions. Their females exchanged natural relations for unnatural, and the males likewise gave up natural relations with females and burned with lust for one another. Males did shameful things with males and thus received in their own persons the due penalty for their perversity.* Romans 1:25-28

This passage is significant because it looks like an unarguable condemnation of both male and female homosexuality (it is the only text in the Bible which addresses lesbians in any way at all, and notice that they get mentioned first!). It is also unspecific about the sexual acts involved. So it appears to rule out every-thing, not just the male-male anal penetration which so preoc-cupied the author of Leviticus. It seems to be dealing, for the first time in the Bible, with the phenomenon of homosexuality per se, rather than just particular sexual acts which breach laws designed to protect patriarchal and sexist social structures. It is also significant because it is a New Testament text and so, for Christians, is clearly binding in a way that the Old Testament texts are not.

To listen to some Christian leaders talk about this passage you would think what we have here is St Paul writing a big chunk of text specifically about how wicked it is to be gay. Actually it is nothing of the sort.

Homosexuality is not the crime, it is the punishment

The key to understanding this oft quoted passage is verse 25. What Paul is doing here is to criticise the idolatry of the non-Jewish world, and especially the Greek and Roman worlds. Indeed the whole of this chapter is designed to condemn not gays but Gentiles (anybody who is not Jewish). And Paul is particularly keen to attack them for the very specific reason that they are irredeemably and incorrigibly idolatrous. What Paul really detests is not homosexuality but idolatry. Outside the Jewish community people worshipped all sorts of idols, objects and animals rather than the 'one true God'. Paul regarded such behaviour as wicked, immoral and perverse. After all, he argues, the true nature of God is apparent to anybody who looks around them and can see the evidence of His handiwork in creation. Therefore these people are culpable. They have deliberately and wilfully suppressed the truth. They know the real God (i.e. the God of Israel) and yet they do not glorify him as they should. They do not honour and worship him but instead they become vain and arrogant. And in their conceit they have abandoned the real eternal living God and replaced him with perishable animals and objects, 'worshipping the creature rather than the creator'. They are guilty of a grave sin, of 'exchanging the truth of God for a lie', and deserve to be punished.

Of course we might want to take issue with the assertion that anyone who looks around and about can 'obviously' see the work of the 'one true God' but that is not the point. St Paul believed this and he also believed that this 'obvious' one true God punished such wicked idolators. And one of God's main punishments was to hand them over to 'degrading passions'. This clearly makes homosexuality the punishment, not the crime.

To make this crystal clear, it may be helpful to draw an analogy with obesity. Being obese is not in itself sinful in any way. What might be regarded as sinful is not obesity itself but the greed and gluttony which inexorably lead to it. People who criticise very overweight individuals may think they look unsightly, unattractive or even ridiculous, but their real criticism is directed toward the individual's self-indulgent lack of restraint which caused the pounds to pile on. In an exactly similar way St Paul thinks homosexuals are shameful, even ridiculous, like a man with long hair, but the sin he is targeting is the idolatry which he believes leads to it.

Homosexuality does not itself therefore call for any punishment. It is just the punishment for something else.

Reasons for doubt

What St Paul seems to be saying is that God made the Gentiles gay as a punishment because He was angry that they did not worship Him but rather worshipped His creatures. There are two questions we might reasonably ask at this juncture:

(1) Does this not sound a lot like the wrathful, vengeful God of the Old Testament and not very much like the Loving God of Jesus and the New Testament?

(2) Are we really to believe that all LGBT people are fundamentally idolatrous and this is why they are gay?

The answers to these questions are self-evident.

(1) Yes it does. And yet Jesus was constantly at pains to stress the love of God. This passage in St Paul's letter really does seem to be odds with that. The picture of God which Jesus presents is of an endlessly forgiving and merciful God who wants only to welcome people into His kingdom of justice and compassion. All Christ's parables about the Kingdom of God always reflect this idea of eternal welcome and invitation to all. Just think of the prodigal son, the good Samaritan, or the lost sheep. They are all about outcasts and sinners who are welcomed into the Kingdom. They are

certainly not about outcasts being subjected to further punishment.

(2) No, we cannot follow St Paul here. Whereas greed and gluttony always produce obesity by the simple laws of nature and physiology there is absolutely no corresponding connection between idolatry and homosexuality. If you eat too many calories you definitely will get fat. If you commit idolatry you will not become gay. I suspect most LGBT people would be hard put to say what idolatry is, let alone be wallowing in their enjoyment of it. The idea that their gayness is due to their worship of false gods and idols is in this sense literally meaningless. Some Christian leaders, following St Paul, try to say that LGBT people are guilty of idolatry even though they do not know it. They cite for example a hedonistic lifestyle as one such false god. Their problem, however, is that a hedonistic lifestyle is character- istic of many people who are not gay. Why has God chosen not to punish these people with homosexuality? And of course there are many gay people who do not have a hedonistic lifestyle either. There are for example many gay Christians who lead exemplary and devout lives. Why then has God chosen to punish them by making them gay? Furthermore, it is the experience of most LGBT people that they grew up gay and have been gay as long as they can remember. They were never anything else and were therefore never in a position to commit idolatry prior to being made gay by God as a punishment. This argument simply will not do.

There are thus both theological and practical grounds for seriously doubting that St Paul's theory can possibly be correct.

St Paul does not see homosexuality as sinful
A crucial fact overlooked by many who use this passage to attack

LGBT people is that in it St Paul does not use the language of sin to describe homosexual behaviour. He does not say that it is sinful. He says that it is shameful. The Greek word translated as 'degrading' is *'atimia'*. In other letters Paul uses this same word to describe varying kinds of disgrace, for example a man who wears his hair long. Homosexuality is therefore seen by Paul as a social dishonour, not as a sin. Here is more proof that it is the punishment for the sin, not the sin itself for which punishment is due.

This point is really very important indeed. Unlike contemporary Christian opponents of LGBT human rights, St Paul does not see homosexuality as evil in itself. It is noteworthy that later in the passage St Paul excludes from the long list of 'things which are not to be done' (which the idolatrous Gentiles do, and which 'are worthy of death') any mention of homosexuality.

And just as they did not see fit to acknowledge God any longer, God gave them over to a depraved mind to do those things that are not proper, being filled with all unrighteousness, wickedness, greed, evil; full of envy, murder, strife, deceit; they are gossips, slanderers, haters of God, insolent, arrogant, boastful, inventors of evil, disobedient to parents, without understanding, untrustworthy, unloving, unmerciful; and although they know the ordinance of God, that those who practise such things are worthy of death, they not only do the same, but give hearty approval to those who practise them. 1 Romans 28-32

For St Paul, these are the things which provoke God's wrath and for which the due punishment is death. It is highly significant that there is here in this list of sins absolutely no reference to homosexuality. Again we might raise the odd eyebrow in relation to some of these sins: are we really to believe that a loving God wants gossips and disobedient children to be put to death? But that is not the point. Whether we agree or not, St Paul clearly believes these acts to be extremely sinful. He does not believe the same of homosexuality.

What he does believe is that homosexual lust brings disgrace and social embarrassment. The Greek word he uses for 'shameful' is *'aschemosyne'*. Being given over to homosexual behaviour is for Paul an embarrassment or a social impropriety rather than something inherently sinful. It is like being found naked in a public situation, 'being caught with your trousers down', as we might say nowadays. Literally it means 'not according to form', and it is related to the English word 'scheme'. *Aschemosyne* is something not in the scheme of things, something which is 'bad form' as used to be said. It dishonours you, robs you of respect, brings you into contempt and ridicule, but it does not define you as evil.

St Paul conflates homosexuality with pederasty
It is also important to bear in mind that when St Paul thought about two men engaged in sexual activity, he was not thinking of consensual loving same sex relationships between two equal individuals. What he mainly had in mind was the widespread practice in Gentile societies, especially Greece and Rome, of pederasty. It was common for older, higher status and more powerful males to engage in homosexual sex, particularly anal intercourse, with younger, lower class men, boys and slaves.

Such activity was broadly accepted as customary and unexceptionable. Often this practice involved a degree of violence, coercion, or at least an absence of consent, and was not uncommonly directed against boys who would now be defined as clearly underage. These facts, of which St Paul was manifestly aware, make it even odder for modern ears to hear that he thought God deliberately caused it to happen. Again this forces us to put a question mark over the extent to which we can simply accept what St Paul believed as either correct or moral, even if we regard ourselves as Christians or followers of Jesus. These facts also further imply that this Pauline text has absolutely nothing to say about the morality of consensual same sex love between adults.

St Paul did not see homosexuality as unnatural

Many people say that homosexuality is 'unnatural'. Actually, it is perfectly natural in the sense that it is part of nature and is observable in animals of all species, just as it has been known in every human society across time and space. Something so ubiquitous, pervasive and resilient cannot logically be said to be unnatural. What these (heterosexual) people usually mean is that they do not like it, do not understand it and want to put it beyond the pale.

Enter once more St Paul. Religious people often appeal to this passage from Romans 1 to buttress their claim that same sex erotic activity is unnatural.

The Greek phrase used by St Paul in this passage translated as 'unnatural' is *'para physin'*, which although often translated as 'against nature' actually means 'beyond nature'. Again we can learn a lot about what Paul had in mind by looking at where else he uses the same phrase. For instance he uses it to refer to grafting a wild branch onto a cultivated tree (a metaphor for God's plan of including Gentiles in the plan of salvation for the Jews). He sees this as 'unnatural' (*para physin*) because cultivated branches are usually grafted onto wild trees rather than the other way round. He naturally saw the Jews as cultivated and the Gentiles as 'wild'. This does mean of course that he sees God in this instance as acting 'unnaturally'! More importantly for the present argument, however, is that it implies homosexuality is unusual rather than wicked.

One interpretation of Paul's use of the phrase *'para physin'* is that, in his culture, it was assumed that everybody is naturally heterosexual, and therefore those who engage in homosexual conduct are acting against or beyond their normal heterosexual nature. In this perspective homosexuality then boils down, in essence, to heterosexuals behaving badly.

This though raises two questions:

(1) why would naturally heterosexual people who are attracted to the opposite sex choose to have sex with people of the same sex to whom they are not attracted?

(2) if it could be shown that some people are not naturally heterosexual but are in fact naturally homosexual would that then make homosexual sex natural and acceptable?

In relation to the first question, the clear answer seems to be that they would not choose to have sex with their own gender rather than the opposite gender. What would be the point? But if everyone were naturally heterosexual, you would not get the amount of homosexuality which we know exists and which has been documented. You might find it in exceptional situations used as a poor substitute (single sex schools, ships, prisons etc) but not in the world at large where the opposite sex is available. Obviously, therefore, some people are 'naturally' homosexual. They just are 'that way'. And so in relation to the second question some Christian churches now accept this but still refuse to recognise that such natural homosexuality is acceptable. However, when they try to defend this position they get themselves into an awful mess.

St Paul's letter to the Romans does not support current church teaching

Current catholic teaching, for example, accepts that some people have a 'homosexual orientation' but warns that: *Although the particular inclination of the homosexual person is not a sin, it is a more or less strong tendency ordered toward an intrinsic moral evil; and thus the inclination itself must be seen as an objective disorder.............Christians who are homosexual are called to a chaste life.* Letter on the pastoral care of homosexual persons from the Congregation for the Doctrine of the Faith (1986).

The Vatican congregation responsible for this teaching claims biblical support from St Paul's letters but it is difficult to see how this can be true. As we have seen, Paul thinks God gave the Gentiles a homosexual orientation as a punishment. But according to current catholic teaching, the orientation itself is neutral, so for the punishment to be a punishment the Gentiles actually have to commit homosexual acts as well as 'be' homosexual. Paul evidently thinks that once God has given you over to homosexual lust the drive to act out the homosexual desires is in general irresistible. Remember he condemns the Gentiles for their acts, not for their failure to resist their desires. If it were possible to resist there would be no shame, no disgrace, no punishment. He clearly thinks it is not possible. He does not find their guilt in 'giving in' to homosexual desire but rather in their commission of actual homosexual acts.

As with his view of heterosexual desire St Paul suspects the majority of people are not able to resist. He would prefer that people remained chaste but if they cannot then 'it is better to marry than to burn'.

Paul's letters also assumed that the world would end within a short timeframe. Christ's imminent return was expected at any moment. Therefore nobody was going to be consigned to a lifetime of sexual abstinence. Paul urges celibacy on his followers because 'the time is grown short' and they should devote what little time and energy remained to them to doing the will of the Father in heaven. Going without sex would not last for very long. Celibacy was a short term emergency measure until Jesus' imminent second coming, and even then Paul accepted that many could not manage it. God seemingly gives the gift of celibacy to very few. (Perhaps fewer than has been believed by the Vatican in the light of the clerical child abuse scandals which have come to light in recent years. Supposedly celibate priests clearly were not celibate. Paul would not have been surprised.)

Paul never imagined that people in general could or should live celibate lives for decades on end. And their inability to do this is not due to their sinfulness but simply to their being human. Once again we encounter a terrible irony. A text written by St Paul is deployed by the Christian church to support teaching which amounts to the very reverse of St Paul's intentions and the text's actual meaning.

A remedy for sin and gay marriage

St Paul's recommendation was, then, that those who do not have the capacity for self-restraint should marry. This gives them a legitimate outlet for their sexual passions and prevents them from falling into Satan's grasp and the various sexual sins which tempt mankind. Marriage, in the immortal words of the Book of Common Prayer, is *'a remedy against sin, and to avoid fornication; that such persons as have not the gift of continency might marry, and keep themselves undefiled members of Christ's body'*.

The Church has clearly accepted therefore that heterosexuals need 'a remedy against sin', but it has been reluctant, to say the least, to recognise the parallel need of homosexuals for the same thing. In this sense it has failed in its pastoral duty, although that is putting it very mildly when set against the millennia of Christian persecution of LGBT people. In all countries where the secular authorities have sought to introduce some kind of gay marriage the Christian churches have always been the most vociferous opponents. And yet if they were to look very closely at what St Paul actually says they might recognise the need for some serious rethinking.

In his first letter to the Corinthians, Paul writes: *For I would that all men were even as I myself. But every man hath his proper gift of God, one after this manner, and another after that. I say therefore to the unmarried and widows, it is good for them if they abide, even as I. But if they cannot contain, let them marry: for it is better to marry than to burn.* 1 Corinthians 7:6-9

In arguing that 'every man hath his proper gift of God', St Paul is drawing attention to the diversity of human sexuality. He is implying that each person discovers their sexuality and sexual orientation in a unique way as a gift of God, 'one after this manner, and another after that'. There does seem here to be an implicit recognition just in this passage that not everyone is the same and perhaps, after all, not everyone is 'obviously' heterosexual. Of course if you are heterosexual then you wish naturally that everybody else should be heterosexual too, 'For I would that all men were even as I myself'. But this you must not do. You must respect the differences which God has himself created.

St Paul's concern here is with protecting people from the sin of fornication by providing them with a legitimate channel for the expression of desire. The logic of his argument is that if marriage is the solution for heterosexuals, then it is also the solution for those with other 'gifts of God', lest they also fall into sin by 'burning' without an acceptable outlet. In addressing the 'unmarried' he could be seen as talking to LGBT people, who if 'they cannot contain' (i.e. remain chaste and celibate) then it is better for them to marry. In this passage, therefore, we have a possible future theological justification for gay marriage which it might be hoped will in time become widely known and accepted.

And of course if such a reading of this particular text can be sustained, it would be a delicious irony that this theological justification for gay marriage should be found in the self same chapter of Romans which Christian homophobes constantly use as their supposed number one LGBT 'terror text'!

LGBT Self defence
Summary Sheet D4: St Paul and Living Beyond Nature

1. In his first letter to the Romans Paul is concerned with attacking not homosexuality but idolatry, the worship of created idols, rather than the worship of the creator.

2. Paul thinks Gentile nations are idolatrous and the punishment for their idolatry is to be given over to 'degrading passions'. Homosexuality is thus the punishment and not the crime.

3. This argument is not very convincing because:
   (1) this behaviour sounds more like the vengeful God of the Old Testament than the loving Father in Heaven described by Jesus;
   (2) LGBT people simply are not idolatrous first and then gay as a result.

4. Paul does not say homosexuals are sinful, only shameful and dishonourable, 'like a man wearing his hair long'.

5. Homosexuality is notably absent from the list of sins worthy of death which Paul itemises later in the letter.

6. Paul did not have same sex love in mind at all. He is referring to exploitative Greek and Roman pederasty.

7. Even pederasty he did not see as unnatural. The phrasing he uses implies that it is just unusual.

8. Paul's preferred option for all men gay or straight is celibacy, but he never expected that anybody would have to endure life-long abstinence because he thought the world would end during his lifetime, with the return of Christ.

9. Paul's concept of marriage is of a 'remedy against sin'.

10. Paul's letter to the Corinthians implies that there are diverse sexualities – 'every man has his proper gift of God, one after this manner and another after that' – but suggests they all

need a remedy against sin. Some see in this a theological justification for gay marriage.

The Defensive Testament Chapter D5

St Paul and Pederasty

What did St Paul mean?

The other frequently cited anti-gay 'terror' text occurs in St Paul's first letter to the Corinthians, chapter 6: *Do you not know that the unjust will not inherit the kingdom of God? Do not be deceived; neither fornicators nor idolaters nor adulterers nor boy prostitutes nor practising homosexuals nor thieves nor the greedy nor drunkards nor slanderers nor robbers will inherit the kingdom of God.* 1 Corinthians 6:9-10

This is seemingly a quite straightforward list of those who will not be getting to heaven unless they change their ways and repent of their sins. The big problem, however, is that although modern biblical translations include in this list 'boy prostitutes' and 'practising homosexuals' it is far from clear that what we understand by these words now is what St Paul actually meant then. Furthermore there is no agreement amongst translators as to what St Paul meant either, and the translations of these terms are varied and have changed over time as social attitudes to sexual matters have altered.

Another problem is that there were many perfectly good words to describe homosexual activity which were used in discussion of it by contemporary writers in New Testament times but which St Paul chose not to use. One can only ask why not? Instead he chose to use words which present formidable challenges to understanding.

The Greek words translated in the modern Biblical text as 'boy prostitutes' and 'practising homosexuals' are *'malakoi'* and *'arsenokoitai'*. There are formidable difficulties with both of them. *'Malakoi'* has a relatively clear meaning in ordinary usage but here Paul seems to be employing it in a novel and strange way. *'Arsenokoitai'* did not exist as a word prior to its appearance in this list. There are no recorded uses of it before Paul's usage in this epistle. And its meaning is therefore uncertain.

Malakos

Malakos is a common and masculine Greek word which definitely means 'soft'. So possibly in this unusual context it implies effeminacy, a characteristic despised in the culture of the ancient world where men were supposed to be tough, firm and in control. St Paul's use of it here seems to be about men failing to act like men; it does not say anything about 'practising homosexuals' or 'boy prostitutes'.

Early English translations implied that *malakos* meant weakness and degeneracy, often rendering it as some version of 'weakling'. From Elizabethan times to the twentieth century it was mostly translated as 'effeminate'. And then, as the previously unknown concept of the 'homosexual' began to develop in the nineteenth century, the translation moved more towards a specific sexual orientation and *malakos* became 'sodomite', 'male prostitute', or 'homosexual pervert'.

This change from *malakos* being translated as 'weak, feeble or unmanly' to its modern translation as 'homosexual' occurred because of shifting social attitudes not through any biblical research. In fact linguistic research into the meaning of *malakos* confirms the earlier rather than the later translations. The word is widely used in ancient literature and its meaning as 'soft' is obvious and undisputed. The softness denoted can apply to objects or to people. Applied to males it highlights their feminine characteristics, which in the ancient world were naturally assumed to be affected deportment, feebleness, fearfulness and lack of courage.

It is though by no means certain that these 'soft' men engaged in homosexual practice. While they might have appeared to be over feminised this does not mean that they allowed themselves to be penetrated by other men. Dale Martin points out that throughout the ancient literature *malakoi* are: *men who live lives of decadence and luxury. They drink too much wine, have too much sex, love gourmet food, and hire professional cooks..... a man may be accused of malakia if he is weak in battle, enjoys, luxury, or is reluctant to commit suicide.* Martin (2006) p.45

Indeed, *malakos* could also mean those men who 'prettied themselves up' in order to attract female sexual partners. Martin comments: *Chariton, in his novel 'Chaereas and Callirhoe', provides a typical portrait of an effeminate man: he has a fresh hairdo, scented with perfume; he wears eye makeup, a soft (malakon) mantle, and light, swishy slippers; his fingers glisten with rings. Only a modern audience would find it strange that he is off to seduce not a man but a maiden.* Op cit p.31

There was therefore in the ancient world no necessary connection between being effeminate and having what we would now call a homosexual orientation, or indeed between being very masculine and having a heterosexual orientation. In Plato's *Symposium*, where there is discussion of the different types of love, man for woman, man for man, woman for woman, it is just taken for granted that male-male love is the most manly. Similarly, in Plutarch's *Dialogue on Love* suggests that men whose orientation is heterosexual show their softness, weakness and effeminacy (*malakia*) by being controlled by women.

Masculine virtues were highly prized and considered by the ancients to be far superior to feminine characteristics which were despised and disparaged. As we have seen in the analysis of Old Testament texts in previous chapters, women in patriarchal societies occupied an inferior position and had few rights. They were controlled by men. What mattered to men in ancient times was preserving their status as men, and this depended on being strong, active, and most importantly of all, in control. These virtues were not at all threatened by male-male sexual activity.

What ancient men had a horror of was not homosexuality but being put in the position of women and not being in control. Dale Martin (ibid) reports the case of Epictetus who praises the actions of an athlete who chose death rather than undergo an operation to save his life by amputating his diseased genital organs. Epictetus thinks this was the right decision because it would be intolerable to go on living without being fully a man.

It is certain that St Paul shared these values. What probably offended his moral sensibilities was not so much the idea of a male-male sexual act but more the idea of a man behaving as a woman. As we have seen in the analysis of Leviticus 18:22 the sin is not males having sex together but males acting as females. Paul Veyne comments: *The passive homosexual was not rejected for his homosexuality but for his passivity, a very serious moral, or rather political infirmity. The passive individual's effeminacy was not the result of his perversion, far from it: it was simply one of the results of his lack of virility, and this was still a vice, even where no homosexuality was present. Roman society never bothered to ask if people were homosexual or not, but it devoted an excessive scrutiny to tiny details of dress, speech, gesture and deportment in furthering its contempt for whose who showed a lack of virility, whatever their sexual tastes.* Veyne (1985) p. 30

St Paul's use of the word *malakos* could well therefore carry no sexual implication whatsoever. It could just be a disapproval of softness in men which betokens an anathematised feminisation. Men can behave as women in many different ways without engaging in sexual activity.

Thus it is perfectly possible that the crime being referred to in St Paul's second letter to the Corinthians is the Leviticus 'abomination' and for St Paul the penalty is death in the life to come, i.e. exclusion from the Kingdom of God, from heaven. Paul was a Jew by birth and a religious scholar steeped in the Hebrew Scriptures. Even if he did have homosexual intercourse partly in mind it could well be that, like the author of Leviticus, what mattered to him most was the after effect on the men involved, i.e. their taboo feminisation, the contamination and corruption of their masculinity.

Again we have to ask those who persist in claiming, against all the evidence, that St Paul was here condemning homosexual practice, why there is no mention of lesbians. We know from his letter to the Romans that he was aware of the existence of gay women. If this passage is really about homosexuality he would surely have included a reference to lesbians as well.

The potency of Paul's condemnation of *malakoi* depends entirely on a grossly unjust system of patriarchal male domination which oppressed and marginalised women. Since we would now find the values of such a culture utterly objectionable and unacceptable we must also reject the condemnation which it gives rise to. In one sense this has in fact 'automatically' happened. In ancient times, and right up to the Reformation, it was entirely credible to Christians that 'effeminates' were an offence against the divinely ordered nature of things and so destined for hell. But this is no longer credible. Nobody now thinks that effeminacy is sinful. We have a priori in fact rejected St Paul's statement. Many of the great male icons of Western culture, actors, authors, artists, comedians, entertainers of all sorts, have been decidedly unmasculine in their appearance and behaviour but have been much loved and cherished by the public at large who would be greatly distressed by the idea of their burning in hell for all eternity.

If the church authorised translators of the Bible had not changed the traditional rendering of *malakoi* as 'effeminate' to a term denoting sexual perversion a great deal of trouble for LGBT people could have been avoided.

The church authorities had a problem of course. If nobody any longer believed that 'effeminates' were excluded from the Kingdom of Heaven, then it looked as though St Paul was wrong. And from the nineteenth century onwards there was also increasing religious anxiety about the emerging concept of a distinct class of person, 'the homosexual'. Put these two things together and the solution is obvious: change the translation, save St Paul, and make it look like he is condemning a hated group. (Bob's your uncle, as they say).

The difficulty for the church authorities now is that too many people know that this is what they have done, and there has been a consequent loss of credibility in this passage as justification for the 'traditional' teaching that God condemns homosexual acts. It is tragic that suicides have occurred because young gay people believed themselves to be evil on the basis of reading these church translations of St Paul's texts. Jeffrey John, for example, writes: *I have a vivid memory of spending an unhappy afternoon some years ago over a Bible trying to talk Simon out of attempting suicide again. Simon was a gay Evangelical student, totally convinced on the basis of (St Paul) that if he ever succumbed to his feelings he would be damned. He had consulted the vicar of his own church, who had promptly prayed for 'healing', and simultaneously ordered him to give up helping in the Sunday School, 'to protect the little boys'. Not surprisingly, Simon had come back to college and swallowed half a bottle of pills. It was particularly tragic for him, and still is for many gay evangelicals, that so many would-be 'Bible Christians' seem to have made a hard line on this issue practically a test of faith.* John (1993) p.7.

(See also Alison (2003) p 100 and Jennings (2005) p vii). In this sense still not enough people know what the church has done. Every young person growing up lesbian, gay, bisexual or trans-gendered needs to know.

Arsenokoitai

To all intents and purposes this is a word which St Paul invented. There are no recorded usages before its appearance in this text. *Arsenokoitai* appears to be made up of two words : *arsen* meaning man or male and *koite* meaning bed. Caution needs to be exercised though in drawing conclusions from this analysis. Some commentators have simply jumped straight to the conclusion that St Paul is 'obviously' talking here about men having sex with men in a bed. This is a completely invalid approach. You cannot elicit the meaning of a word by analysing its constituent parts. Blackmail is not black mail.

So whereas *malakoi* had a definite meaning ascertainable from studying its previous uses in published texts prior to the time of St Paul *arsenokoitai* has no such history.

Some commentators have suggested that they form a pair and derive their meaning from each other. Thus *arsenokoitai* would be the active partner and *malakoi* the passive partner in an act of homosexual anal intercourse. This though is merely an assumption which at the very least is unlikely to be the whole story. As we have seen, we can be fairly sure that *malakos* does not properly mean anything other than 'soft', and at most in this context 'effeminate' (of which sexual passivity would be only a small element and need not be implicated at all). And as we shall see, nobody can be certain of what *arsenokoitai* means because St Paul dreamed it up himself. Also this Pauline text is not made up of pairs of terms, so there does not seem to be a basis for treating just these two words as if they were a pair.

The meaning of *arsenokoitai* is then unknown, but the context in which St Paul employs the word does though afford some clues.

In the first part of 2 Corinthians chapter 6 Paul is criticising Christians in Corinth for taking each other to court to settle their disputes. He says this means that they are offering themselves up for judgement by the unjust, presumably because the judges in these courts were not Christians. He says they should appoint one of their own to decide judgements and not resort to the civil courts. He goes so far as to say that they should put up with injustice and suffer in silence. By going to court they have already failed as Christians, and actually commit an injustice against their fellow Christians. So this whole text is about injustice and doing wrong to others.

When we arrive at verse 6, Paul declares that the unjust will not inherit the Kingdom of God and then lists ten kinds of unjust people who will be excluded. All of these in their own way inflict some kind of injury, wrong or injustice on other people. The two words in the ten which are not clear are of course *malakoi* and *arsenokoitai* but we must assume that Paul thought they were involved in causing damage to others in some way, and that his readers would understand this.

It is unlikely therefore that Paul had simple same sex love in mind for either word. Much more likely is the Leviticus context discussed earlier. Dale Martin (2006) notes that a contemporary of Paul's, Philo, like him also familiar with both Greek and Hebrew cultures, had no hesitation in seeing the Leviticus proscriptions as targeting the Greek and Roman practice of pederasty. Philo was against the practice because it feminised one of the partners and corrupted the male nature of both: *'Mark how conspicuously they braid and adorn the hair of their heads, and how they scrub and point their faces with cosmetics and pigments and the like, and smother themselves with fragrant unguents.......These persons are rightly judged worthy of death by those who obey the law, which ordains that the man-woman (androgynos) who debases the sterling coin of nature should perish unavenged.... And the lover of such may be assured that he is subject to the same penalty....... He sees no harm in becoming a tutor and instructor in the grievous vice of unmanliness (anandrias) and effeminacy (malakias) by prolonging the bloom of the young and emasculating the flower of their prime, which should rightly be trained to strength and robustness.'* (Special Laws 111 37-39). If this is also a characterisation of how Paul saw pederasts then we have the explanation of why they are in the list of the unjust. The *arsenokoitai* harms the *malakoi* by corrupting him and robbing him of his manliness. The *malakoi* harms himself by behaving as a woman. They both deserve death, now or in the world to come. What is crucial for LGBT people today, however, is that the *arsenokoitai* and the *malakoi* are not excluded by Paul because they are homosexuals. There is not even any condemnation of pederasty as a sexual act. The sole concern is that men should not be identified with the despised category of women.

The theologian Dale Martin has undertaken a study of subsequent uses of the word *'arsenokoitai'* after the time of St Paul. In a detailed analysis of texts he notes something particularly odd. As in the epistle to the Corinthians, it mostly figures in lists of sinners, but not quite where it might be expected to appear. It tends to crop up in lists of 'financial' sins such as economic injustice, exploitation, fraud, accepting corrupt gifts, extortion, withholding wages, oppression of the poor. And it tends to be lacking from those vice lists concerned with sexual peccadilloes, such as adultery and prostitution. He concludes that: *it is used to mean some kind of economic exploitation, probably by sexual means: rape or sex by economic coercion, prostitution, pimping or something of that sort'* Martin (2006) p. 41

What appears to be the case is that the primary 'sin' is the damaging treatment of other people, with any sexual activity being a secondary or subsidiary consideration, more the means by which the sin is committed rather than being the sin itself. This would in fact reflect New Testament values where every action is to be judged according to how far it promotes the love of God and the love of neighbour. The meaning of this word seems then very far from a simple straightforward condemnation of homosexuality or same-sex love. To use it for this purpose looks to be quite unwarranted.

The word *arsenokoitai* occurs once more in the New Testament in Paul's first letter to Timothy, once again in a list of sins. Paul writes that the law is laid down: *..not for the just, but for the lawless and disobedient, the impious and sinners, for the irreligious and godless, for parricides and matricides, for fornicators, arsenokoitai,* *slave traders, liars, perjurers and whatever else is contrary to sound teaching.* 1Timothy 1:10

Scroggs (1983 p.120) has pointed out that the word which follows *arsenokoitai* in this passage, translated here as slave traders, is *andrapodistes,* which can just as well be translated as 'kidnappers'. Slave traders would often be involved in kidnapping slaves, and sometimes this would be in order to furnish prostitutes to work in brothels. Its position between fornicators and slave kidnappers may suggest that *arsenokoitai* here describes the men who visited brothels in order to avail themselves of the services of boy prostitutes.

If this is correct, then once again we are dealing with sexual exploitation and not with anything remotely approaching same sex love as that is understood today.

Ultimately only St Paul can know fully what he had in mind in creating this word. But what we can say for sure is that the certainty with which some Christian leaders declare that 'obviously' what Paul meant was men who have sex with men is totally unjustified and spurious.

LGBT Self defence
Summary Sheet D5: St Paul and Pederasty

1. St Paul's first letter to the Corinthians presents a list of the 'unrighteous' who will not get into heaven but the translations of *malakoi* and *arsenokoitai* as 'boy prostitutes' and 'practising homosexuals' in modern bibles are highly suspect.

2. *Malakoi* means soft. Applied to men it means effeminate and unmanly. It has no direct sexual meaning.

3. Effeminate men before the modern era often had a heterosexual orientation.

4, Homosexual activity between men in the ancient world did not threaten their manliness but was considered normal male behaviour, especially in Greek and Roman culture.

5. Paul is following Leviticus here in objecting to men behaving as women and being weak and passive.

6. If this is supposed to be a condemnation of same sex activity why is there no condemnation of lesbians? It is therefore no such thing.

7. The church authorities changed the translation to make it look like St Paul was condemning gay men once the category of homosexual emerged in the 19th/20th centuries.

8. *Arsenokoitai* is a word made up by St Paul. Nobody can be sure what it means. He did not use the perfectly good words for homosexuals available at the time.

9. After St Paul, *arsenokoitai* came to mean some kind of exploitation involving sexual means.

10. The real sin here is not sex but damaging other people, i.e. not loving God and neighbour. This text has nothing to do with consensual same sex love.

The Defensive Testament Chapter D6

Being Possessed

The exorcism of Richard Kirker

At the 1998 Lambeth Conference, the meeting of all the primates of the Anglican Communion which takes place once every ten years, two things happened which were of great significance for LGBT people. The first was the passing of the infamous Resolution 1.10 which declared that the Anglican Church 'rejects homosexual practice as incompatible with scripture' and the second was the attempted exorcism of Richard Kirker by Bishop Emmanuel Chukwama of Nigeria.

Resolution 1.10 marked a watershed in the development of Anglican attitudes towards LGBT people. It has become a sort of magisterial teaching from a church that has no magisterium, that has no centralised, formalised dogmatic teaching system such as the Roman Catholic Church has. No magisterium perhaps, but this teaching has nonetheless exercised a baleful influence over the lives of LGBT people, both inside and outside the church, because it has been the governing principle directing the voting behaviour of Anglican bishops in the House of Lords. It played a part, for example, in the decision of many of them to oppose equality legislation in the United Kingdom, designed to provide protection from discrimination, for LGBT people. This was a manifesto commitment of the governing Labour Party in 2005. In 2010 some bishops, who of course are not elected, successfully frustrated the equal rights plans of politicians, who had been democratically elected.

What this odious little teaching means, in effect, is that if you are lesbian or gay there is something wrong with you. Scripture is supposedly a unified and coherent account, without any internal contradiction, of God's plan for His creation. There is no place for gays in this account and therefore if you are homosexual you are flawed. You are a defective heterosexual because God only makes heterosexuals. Some Christians see this defect as being caused by the Devil and his evil spirits who have entered you and taken possession of you. It is these evil spirits which drive you to feel supposedly perverted lust and to commit supposed abominations abhorrent in the sight of God. These Christians believe the only way to save LGBT people is to exorcise the demons within. Exorcism can supposedly expel evil spirits and leave the erstwhile gay person as a pure heterosexual as God apparently intended all along.

Bishop Emmanuel Chukwama is one such Christian. Believing that there on that Summer's day at the University of Kent campus he was meeting the embodiment of Satanic perversion in the shape of Richard Kirker, who is a deacon of the Church of England and founder of the Lesbian and Gay Christian movement, and who was there protesting against Anglican homophobia, the good bishop set about his task. He did this in the public gaze of the crowd and the full glare of the media circus gathered for the conference. And he did it not once, but three times, haranguing the poor deacon in a most alarming way.

Now there is a double bind in this exorcism business. If the exorcism does not work then that is your fault, not the exorcist's. You are simply too steeped in sin and wickedness. We can only conclude that Richard Kirker must be very wicked indeed since his exorcism did not work in the sense that of course he was not 'cured' of being gay, and exorcists don't come much more high ranking than a bishop!

Jesus was possessed

What these exorcising Christians would do well to meditate on is the fact that their view of LGBT people as 'possessed' is exactly the same as the view that the Jewish religious authorities of the time took of Jesus. They thought there was something wrong with him. They thought he was deviant, defective and possessed by evil spirits. *And the scribes which came down from Jerusalem said,"he hath Beelzebub".* Mark 10:22

Beelzebub is one of the more active demons in Satan's hierarchy, famously going on to have a starring role in the dreadful business of the witch trials of Salem in the Massachusetts of 1692. By saying that Jesus is possessed by Beelzebub the religious authorities simultaneously achieve three things:

1. they undermine his teaching which challenged their comfortable orthodoxy;
2. they confirm themselves as the source of what is good, right and normal;
3. they make him an outcast and threaten his wellbeing and continued existence.

Like Richard Kirker, Jesus was bringing a message which the established authorities did not want to hear and which they would seek to destroy with both symbolic and actual violence. In the Gospel of Luke we read of an attempt actually to kill Jesus to stop him preaching: *When they heard this, all in the synagogue were filled with rage. They got up, drove him out of the town, and led him to the brow of the hill on which their town was built, so that they might hurl him off the cliff.* Luke 4:28-29

Even Jesus' family do not support him. They think he is crazy too. They try to restrain him. *And when his family and friends heard of it, they went out to lay hold on him: for they said, "he is beside himself".* Mark 3: 21. *They were scandalised by him.* Mark 6:3. *For neither did his brethren believe in him.* John 7:5

Once again, there is an all too frequent and sad parallel with the lives of LGBT people. Being gay is essentially just a natural minority human variant, like being left handed. But growing up and realising that you are gay, you find yourself surrounded by a hostile and uncomprehending world. When you try and speak the truth of who and what you are, and say that you are just as normal and human as everyone else, your truth is not believed and a gross untruth is forced upon you, even by your family. Your family may not believe you but rather believe the author- ities of the time. And whether these authorities be religious, judicial or medical, they all defend the heterosexist ideology that denies your existence and condemns you as evil or sick. Over the centuries sons and daughters without number have been evicted from families who side with heterosexist institutions rather than believe their own children. "You're no son of mine" is the iconic phrase which captures this unspeakable tragedy of truly colossal proportions.

This is why Jesus put so much emphasis on belief. The only real purpose you have as a human being is to seek out truth and believe in it, whatever the cost. I am sure that Bishop Chukwama does believe in Jesus and does believe that Jesus is truth. It is just such a pity that people like him cannot see that with all their talk of spirits and demons they are simply reproducing exactly the same oppressive ideological apparatus which was used to suppress the truth of Jesus, and that is tragically ironical. Ultimately of course the authorities of first century Palestine did not succeed. Truth will out, as they say. Christ's truth has become known to the whole world. In a similar way, despite all the centuries of cruel persecution, the truth of the humanity of gay people is gradually being recognised and believed in. We need to work for the day when there will be no more casting out of sons and daughters, and no more exorcising of supposed demons.

What was Jesus doing when he cast out demons?

So what was Jesus doing when we are told that he cast out demons? If you think about the people who were afflicted with demons in the New Testament, they were often individuals whose social situation had left them subject to immense stress resulting in behavioural disorders which today would be diagnosed as forms of mental illness. The biblical scholar, Paul Hollenbach (1981), has argued that such people were the victims of 'class antagonisms rooted in economic exploitation, conflicts, between traditions where revered traditions are eroded, colonial domination and revolution.' The experience of brutal oppression by the occupying Roman forces had profoundly disrupted Israelite society and cast many Jewish peasants adrift. As Goss (1993) has noted, political oppression generates an 'oppression sickness that fractures personal and social structures of meaning' (p.99). In this state, the social integrity of groups and the psychological integrity of individuals collapse, creating widespread anomie, alienation and a general sense of bewildering purposelessness and meaninglessness. The disturbing and challenging behaviour patterns which emerge as a result are then labelled by the powerful dominant elite as evidence of demon possession. This definition then justifies the existing unequal and dysfunctional status quo, and with it both the privileged position of the powerful and the excluded position of the outcast.

Through this kind of social psychological analysis, it is possible to see that what Jesus was really doing was to challenge those with power in the Jewish religious establishment which had accommodated itself to, and cooperated with, the Roman occupying forces. He refused to accept that the people brought to him were 'evil', but rather recognised the demonic and wicked social system which had caused the distress that underlay the symptoms which they presented. What Jesus was delivering these people from was not so much 'demons' but rather from the all-too-human social structures which had demonised them.

Jesus was well aware that he was not possessed by demons when his family and friends did not like what he was saying and consequently declared that Beelezebub had got into him. We can only imagine that he must also have known also that most of those unfortunate victims labelled as possessed were no more possessed than he was. Jesus' purpose was to announce the coming of the Kingdom of God. The obstacle to the in-breaking of the kingdom was not the poor wretches writhing and foaming in front of him, but rather the greed and wickedness of the powerful who benefited from the unjust social and political structures which had so damaged them.

What Jesus was seeking to do was to release these people from their suffering and pain. He was welcoming them in to the justice and compassion characteristic of the non-alienated loving relationships in the Kingdom of God. These castings out were 'public symbolic actions directed against the political and religious order that produced oppressive sickness' (Goss 1993 p 100). Jesus restored their God-given freedom to be fully themselves.

Possession as social definition
Thus it could be said that people defined as being possessed by demons suffer not so much from demons as from social definitions.

An interesting comparison can be made with the treatment of left-handed people. Being left-handed is associated in many societies and cultures with evil and the Devil. This negativity is reflected in many languages. The latin for left is 'sinister'. The English word 'left' comes from the Old English 'lyft' which means weak, worthless and womanish. The French word 'gauche' also means awkward and inept. The Italian word is 'mancino' which also means dubious and dishonest. In other cultures there are many other negative connotations for 'left' including 'hated' and 'crazy'. By contrast 'right' is good. Right means correct, proper, acceptable. The Greek word 'dexter' which gives the English word 'dextrous' means of course skilful, clever, adept. All that is good and worthy is right; all that is malign and unholy is left.

This social definition of right as good and left as bad is essentially arbitrary but very powerful. In medieval times the left hand was associated with witchcraft, and the Devil was commonly depicted in images with his left hand outstretched. This was literally a process of demonising left-handed people. In some cultures women were forbidden from touching their husband's face with their left hand. For centuries the Christian Church taught that being left-handed branded a person as a servant of the Devil. Anything left handed was regarded as inherently evil. Jesus is assumed to sit on the right hand of God. In pictures of the Last Judgement God points to hell with his left hand showing the left hand side as the demonic and diabolical path to eternal damnation.

Because of this social definition, the treatment of left-handed people throughout history has been atrocious. They have been persecuted, tortured and murdered. Their left-handedness has not been accepted and brutal attempts have been made to force them to become right-handed. Such practices continued even within western education systems into the twentieth century. And yet some of the greatest people who have ever lived have been left handed, including Beethoven, Michaelangelo, Nietzsche, and Leonardo da Vinci. But this has not changed the view that left handed people are somehow unnatural and possessed of the Devil. Only in comparatively recent times has this negative image faded.

The parallel here with gay people is obvious. The percentage of the population reckoned to be gay (between 8% and 15%) is much the same as the percentage of the population thought to be left-handed, and the treatment has been much the same: negative demonising, assumed possession by evil spirits, horrific punishment, forced 'conversion'. In both cases it is self-evident that these are naturally occurring universal human variants which are in this sense perfectly normal. But in both cases they are socially defined as negative, which leads to the presumption of 'possession' and maltreatment. As Jesus understood, the problem is not people possessed by evil spirits but rather the environing social structure which defines them as such.

A key player in the social structures doing the defining is the Church. As we shall see in the next chapter, the way in which the Christian churches arrive at their definitions continues to be a cause for grave concern.

LGBT Self defence
Summary Sheet D6: Being Possessed

1. Two key events at the Lambeth Conference 1998 were:
   (1) the passing of Resolution 1.10 declaring homosexual practice to be incompatible with scripture;
   (2) the 'exorcism' of Richard Kirker, founder of the Lesbian and Gay Christian Movement (LGCM).

2. The claim that LGBT people are possessed by demons or the devil is absurd and archaic. It also ignores the New Testament accounts which show that the Jewish authorities believed Jesus was possessed.

3. Accusations of demon possession are a way of neutralising people whose truth you do not want to hear.

4. Jesus' casting out of demons involved affirming the worth and valued of damaged and downtrodden individuals excluded from society and who as a result suffered symptoms of physical and mental illness.

5. Jesus challenged the cruel and unjust power structures which oppressed and hurt people. He welcomed them into the loving relationships of the Kingdom of God.

6. In this sense, people defined as possessed suffer from social definitions rather than demons.

7. Left-handed people suffered a similar kind of prejudice to LGBT people and were equally defined as evil in the past.

8. Nowadays left-handedness is seen for the natural universal human variant that it is. It is to be hoped that homosexuality will come to be seen in the same way.

The Defensive Testament Chapter D7

Textual Abuse

What is textual abuse?

In this final chapter of the Defensive Testament I should like to raise what may now seem an obvious question: if the so-called 'terror texts' discussed in the previous chapters have nothing to do with homosexuality how do the patriarchal Christian churches manage to use them to condemn homosexuals?

This obvious question has an obvious answer, already hinted at several times: these churches 'abuse' the Biblical texts.

By textual abuse, I mean the deliberately selective interpretation or misinterpretation of isolated biblical texts to give them a decontextualised prejudicial contemporary meaning.

The meaning is decontextualised because it ignores the surrounding social, linguistic and cultural context in which the text was written. The meaning is prejudicial because it is selected solely on the basis of its usefulness in demonising a particular group of people. And the meaning is contemporary because it arises from the present situation in which the church seeks to use it, and not from the past situation in which it originally arose.

The decontextualised contemporary prejudicial meanings extracted from Biblical texts to justify a predetermined negative view then underpin the condemnation, persecution and maltreatment of particular groups of people, which historically has included slaves, black people, Jews, lepers, women, lesbian and gay people, children and the disabled, amongst others.

As Adrian Thatcher (2008) has shown in his study of the Bible as a 'savage text', this sort of textual abuse has been committed by Christian churches of many denominations, right across the ecclesiastical spectrum.

In the following pages we will consider some specific examples of textual abuse perpetrated by three major strands of Christianity:

(1) the Roman Catholic Church
(3) the Protestant fundamentalists of the Evangelical Alliance.
(2) the Anglican Church

(1) The Roman Catholic Church: Homosexualitatis Problema, Letter on the Pastoral Care of Homosexual Persons (1986)

This document was authored by Joseph Ratzinger, the future Pope Benedict XVI, but then head of the Congregation for the Doctrine of the Faith. It begins by referring back to a previous letter written in 1975, *Persona Humana*, which **for the first time** in Catholic teaching introduced the concept of the 'homosexual condition' as separate from homosexual acts. It declared that the 'homosexual condition', or orientation, is in itself neutral but homosexual acts are 'intrinsically disordered' and 'able in no case to be approved of'. In the 1986 letter this position was changed to demonise the orientation itself: *Although the particular inclination of the homosexual person is not a sin, it is a more or less strong tendency ordered toward an intrinsic moral evil; and thus the inclination itself must be seen as an objective disorder.*

This of course is only a whisker away from saying that all gay people are inherently evil. The teaching focuses entirely on physical acts and is based on a crude, impoverished, and hopelessly inadequate understanding of human sexuality. Sexuality is not just about a tendency to 'do' certain acts. It is about desire and delight, wanting to be with someone, to share with them, to feel at ease, to enjoy companionship, to touch, to embrace, to be loyally committed, to participate in mutually reciprocated happiness. This teaching is a shockingly reductionist view of human life. Ratzinger claims to find support for it in the Bible.

(1a) Ratzinger and Sodom

He starts with the story of Sodom and asserts that: *there can be no doubt of the moral judgement made there against homosexual relations..... and (this story) presents homosexual acts as acts of grave depravity.*

This is little more than a glib assertion which does not bear close scrutiny. As we have seen in Chapter D1 there is, on the contrary, every reason to doubt that this text warrants any such damning interpretation of same sex love. Furthermore it is significant that Ratzinger's letter quotes the story as beginning in Genesis 19, when we have already seen it actually begins in chapter 18. By (deliberately?) missing out the first part, where God rewards Abraham's hospitality with a guarantee of posterity in the form of a son, the whole point and significance of Lot's being similarly rewarded for his hospitality with a guarantee of escape from destruction is lost. This manoeuvre enables Ratzinger to deflect attention away from the true significance of the text, which is about rewarding hospitality (love of neighbour) and punishing inhospitality (failure to love neighbour), in order to make his claim that it is about the condemnation of homosexual relations.

From this it is obvious that the anti-gay prejudice precedes his reading of the text, whose real significance he distorts to produce the decontextualised prejudicial contemporary interpretation he wishes to promulgate.

(1b) Ratzinger and Leviticus

Ratzinger's document follows a similarly devious path in its treatment of the two verses in Leviticus which we discussed in chapter D2. He blithely states that: *The author of Leviticus excludes from the people of God those who behave in a homosexual fashion.*

As we have seen, the author of Leviticus does no such thing.

The author of Leviticus addresses only males and so does not exclude 'those who behave in a homosexual fashion' who are female;

The author of Leviticus condemns men behaving as women and the practice of idolatry, not homosexuality;

The author of Leviticus is utterly unconcerned about non-penetrative sexual acts.

Here once again, Ratzinger makes an unjustified sweeping assertion which is tantamount to textual abuse. As Moore (2003) comments: *What is at stake here (in Leviticus) is not a supposed divine plan of heterosexuality, but a supposed divine plan of male dominance. What this law depends on, and what it expresses, is the idea that God wills male superiority over the female; it also depends upon and expresses a conception of sexual penetration as a symbolic actualisation of that superiority. Most modern Christians reject absolutely both of these ideas.* (p.80)

Needless to say, Ratzinger does not even begin to address the problem that there is no reasonable basis for accepting some of the proscriptions of Leviticus and ignoring others. Nor does he deal with the New Testament texts which imply that the Jewish Holiness Code has no relevance to Christians.

Ratzinger's 1986 letter follows on from a long, sad history of abusing these texts. The Vatican Congregation for the Doctrine of the Faith over which Ratzinger presided used to be called the Holy Inquisition. In those days it was not just a question of arguing about the abuse of Biblical texts. Just to make plain its disapproval of homosexuals, the Inquisition sentenced Spanish sodomites to be burned alive, and burned alive 'without benefit of strangulation'.

(1c) Ratzinger and St Paul

The 1986 document also appeals to the commonly cited texts in the epistles of St Paul. The first is found in the letter to the Romans: *They exchanged the truth of God for a lie and revered and worshipped the creature rather than the creator, who is blessed forever. Amen. Therefore, God handed them over to degrading passions. Their females exchanged natural relations for unnatural, and the males likewise gave up natural relations with females and burned with lust for one another. Males did shameful things with males and thus received in their own persons the due penalty for their perversity.* Romans 1 25-27

As we have seen in chapter D4, what Paul is concerned about here is the idolatry of the non-Jewish world. It is idolatry that he rails against throughout the whole chapter, not homosexuality. It is abundantly clear from the text itself that homosexuality is the punishment and not the crime. Ratzinger ignores what is in front of his eyes. He also ignores the scholarship which would tell him very clearly that Paul believed the punishment to consist in shame and social dishonour. The 'degrading passions' idolators suffer are an unpleasant embarrassment for themselves, not something evil or sinful in the sight of God requiring further punishment.

Later in the same chapter in verses 29 to 31 Paul gives his famous list of those who will not enter heaven, implying that these are also the result of being idolatrous, which creates disharmony between the Creator and His creatures. St Paul writes that such people are: *full of all injustice, evil, greed, wickedness, full of envy, murder, quarrelling, treachery, malignity; whisperers, slanderers, God-haters, insolent, haughty, boasters, inventors of evil, disobedient to parents, senseless, covenant breakers, disloyal, inhumane, merciless.*

Considering this list of evil-doers Ratzinger's document declares: *Paul is at a loss to find a clearer example of this disharmony than homosexual relations.*

This is a quite astonishing claim for which no explanation is put forward, and which appears quite unwarranted by the text. It is practically incomprehensible. Ratzinger seems not to have noticed that homosexuals are not mentioned in this list of the excluded, precisely because Paul has already established that their conduct is shameful but not sinful.

One has to ask if the present pope really believes that a loving same sex couple engaged in sexual relations is a clearer example of disharmony with God than murder, treachery or inhumanity? In the light of his 2009 observation that gay people are more of a threat to the future of humanity than the destruction of the rain forests, we might well fear that the answer is yes. But he can only arrive at this conclusion by seriously abusing the Biblical text.

(2) The Protestant fundamentalists of the Evangelical Alliance

The Evangelical Alliance published their pamphlet, *Faith, Hope and Homosexuality*, in 1999. In it they are very clear about their view: *We affirm God's love and concern for all humanity, including homosexual people, but believe homoerotic sexual practice to be incompatible with His will as revealed in Scripture.*

The document's authors acknowledge that the references to homosexuality in the Bible are very few in number, but they do not address the question of why this should be so if it is such a dreadful sin. Why did God say so little and Jesus say nothing at all? This must be surprising to them, given their belief that scripture is everything.

The major problem evangelicals face is trying to import modern values into Biblical texts which do not share them, without appearing to do so. For example, they admit that God gave us 'sex for pleasure' and that the vast majority of sexual acts actually committed are not for procreation (incidentally neither of which would ever have been freely admitted in the past). So if that is now all right with God, where is the argument against homosexuality which rests on its not leading to procreation? On this point they are silent. Similarly, they acknowledge that what they see as God's plan for monogamous marriage (the so-called creation ordinances discussed in chapter D3) is not at all lived out in the rest of the Old or New Testaments, not least in the life of the unmarried Christ himself. But they still believe that the modern 'mum and dad' nuclear family is somehow the 'purposed end' of these texts, without however advancing any credible theory as to how this could be. God plans five thousand years of non-monogamy to produce monogamy now? It seems doubtful, doesn't it?

(2a) The Evangelical Alliance and Sodom

Their view of Sodom and Gomorrah is that it is essentially about a threatened gang rape and therefore not directly relevant to homosexuality as it is understood today. This recognition of the difference between violent rape and consensual sexual love, which would be so obvious in a heterosexual context but is inexplicably somehow so much more difficult for some churches to see in a homosexual context, is nevertheless a move in the right direction. And so well done the Evangelical Alliance for this at least. There is still, however, a failure to see the whole story as essentially about rewarding hospitality in which the threatened gang rape is merely incidental.

(2b) The Evangelical Alliance and Leviticus

In discussing the prohibitions of Leviticus the writers of the Evangelical Alliance document never mention the obvious and well-known historical contextual fact that all of the abominations are essentially to do with the mixing of categories and the infringement of boundaries. They have a singleminded focus on using, or misusing, (or arguably abusing), this text to condemn all homosexual acts, even though what they would call 'the plain sense of the text' only refers to male-male sexual intercourse. For the Evangelical Alliance, the main concern is the supposed threat posed by homosexuality: *All such practices are viewed as a threat to marriage and the family.*

The problem for them though is that the Leviticus text does not say this, and nor is the claim supported anywhere else in the Old and New Testaments. This is a modern preoccupation which they have simply imported and imposed.

Focussing on the Leviticus death penalty prescription, they comment: *The Assyrians may have outlawed forcible same-sex intercourse, and the Egyptians may have banned pederasty, but Israel stood alone in viewing homosexual acts as a whole with this degree of severity.*

But we need to remember that the Evangelical Alliance are biblical fundamentalists. Their position is that this is the inerrant word of God for all time. They believe in the supreme authority of Scripture. Why therefore do they not call for the death penalty for homosexuals as the 'plain sense' of the text demands? On what grounds can they possibly declare, as they do in the conclusion to the Faith, Hope and Homosexuality document, that: *We call upon evangelical congregations to welcome and accept sexually active homosexual people.*

The Biblical text most certainly does not mandate this. Clearly they are doing precisely what they claim not to be doing. They are using the text to defend two preexisting prejudices, neither of which are supported by it: a revulsion against homosexual love and a revulsion against the idea of killing a human being. How is it that 'the plain sense of the text' is to be followed to the letter in one case and then completely ignored in another? As we have seen earlier, there is no Biblical, theological or other basis for deciding to accept some teachings and ignore others, especially if you are a fundamentalist Bible believing Christian.

Of course, what the Evangelical Alliance is trying to do here is to be *nice,* as we understand things now. They do not like homosexuality and they fear it. They think they have found a place in the Bible where God condemns it too. But God goes too far. The Evangelical Alliance is queasy about stoning people to death. They do not seem to realise the logic of their position demands that they had better start looking for pebbles straightaway or God's anger will be turned on them for tolerating the abominable.

(2c) The Evangelical Alliance and St Paul

And when it comes to St Paul they are incredibly nice! They describe his list of transgressions as one that would 'convict most, if not all of us'. They admit that he is concerned with idolatry and they even observe that: *This surely confirms that the church is a community of sinners and disallows the singling out of homosexual sin for special condemnation.*

They further acknowledge that all positions within the debates about sexuality are based on picking and choosing according to prejudices. And yet somehow they still manage to conclude that: *Dispassionate exegesis supports the longstanding prohibition (on homosexuality).*

It does not, of course. The longstanding prohibition rests on mere assertion repeated time and time again thereby coming to take on the feel of a sacred tradition. But LGBT people should take heart from the fact that the Evangelical Alliance have decided to introduce modern humane compassion into their assertions, albeit a procedure which is totally illegitimate in terms of their own view of scripture as totally authoritative. But far better that a church's textual abuse should be aimed at humanising the barbarity of the past, than that it should be employed to add further pain and misery to human lives in the present.

(3) The Anglican Church: Issues in Human Sexuality

The surprising empathy (and sympathy) evinced by the Evangelical Alliance document contrasts sadly with the unsympathetic hard line taken by the Anglican church in its influential document 'Issues in Human Sexuality', referred to henceforth as Issues. You could sum things up as the Evangelicals wanting to say 'we are all sinners' and the Anglicans saying '*you* are all sinners'.

In 1991 the House of Bishops issued a statement under this title essentially declaring homosexual activity to be incompatible with scripture. This was followed in 2003 by a much longer work with the same title, running to some 400 pages, purporting to be a guide to the theological debate on homosexuality. Actually this is less of a guide and more of a heterosexist manifesto.

Many pages in the 2003 document are devoted to how careful it is necessary to be in interpreting scripture. All readings are provisional and partial. You have to understand the linguistic and cultural assumptions built into the text. The meaning of a text is relative to the people interpreting it. The Anglican Church has always stressed the importance of combining a reading of scripture with an understanding of tradition and, most importantly, with the exercise of reason. This is all jolly good stuff and absolutely correct. The only problem is it all seems to fly out of the window as soon as the authors start to talk about the 'terror texts'.

(3a) Anglicans and Sodom

Once they launch into the story of Sodom and Gomorrah they are straight back into trying to turn it into an anti gay text. In relation to both Sodom and the Levite in Gibeah the Bishops had written in the 1991 statement: *What, however, Christians have too often failed to see is that these stories simply are not relevant to the case, say, of two men or two women who find themselves deeply emotionally attracted to one another, and who wish to live together in a sexual relationship for mutual support in every area of their lives. The situations are too far apart in human terms for any ethical transfer to be made.* (p. 14).

This is a totally laudable and unarguably true statement. But the authors of the 2003 document renege on the bishops' position. They obsess over the meaning of the word 'know', devoting two whole pages to proving that it is sexual (which is hardly disputed anyway), and conclude simplistically that the text sees *the sin of the people of Sodom as involving an act of sexual immorality of a homosexual nature.* (p.122).

This is an underhand procedure. Whilst they allow that a condemnation of homosexual rape is not a condemnation of consensual homosexual sex (anymore than the heterosexual equivalents would be) they nonetheless argue that: *Sexual relationships that fall outside the limits that God has laid down are seen as coming under God's judgement.*

This really is unworthy of any Christian, let alone church theologians. It is smearing of the worst possible kind. In the light of Biblical scholarship, the authors of Issues have to accept that the only sexual element in the story is a possible threatened gang rape which has no implication at all for consensual sex. And yet they still want to insinuate (for that is all it is now theologically possible for them to do) that Sodom's destruction by God is due to the orientation of the rape, rather than to its violent and inhospitable character. And they make this nasty insinuation in the full knowledge that in the Old Testament there are many reported 'sexual relationships that fall outside the limits that God has laid down' which do **not** come under divine judgement e.g. the incest between Lot and his daughters discussed earlier. And they totally ignore the whole point of the story which is about reward for looking after your neighbour and punishment for not so doing. The analysis is disingenuous, and is designed solely to give the appearance of solidity to their foundationless homophobic premise. It is a disgraceful piece of propaganda masquerading as Biblical exegesis.

(3b) Anglicans and Leviticus

The authors of Issues act in a similar way with regard to

Leviticus. They appear to be so obsessed with the creation ordinances discussed in chapter D3 that they simply impose their predetermined ideas on the Leviticus prescriptions. They quote Grenz who contends that *The injunctions of the holiness code regulating sexual behaviour appear to have as their intention the safeguarding and preservation of the marital context in which sexual acts are to occur.* (p.125).

This is little more than ideological wishful thinking. It starts from its own deep emotional commitment to the modern nuclear family of mum, dad, 2.4 children and a dog, and reads this back into the totally alien cultural context of a Bronze Age desert society. It glosses over all the inherent difficulties in this procedure we have witnessed before:

(1) As Issues itself notes in its opening remarks on how to read the Bible, but then seems to forget, such revisionist cultural imposition is an entirely illegitimate procedure which produces unconvincing and essentially meaningless results;

(2) The use of the word 'appear to have as their intention' suggests Grenz himself is aware that he is engaged in a dubious interpretive practice;

(3) As we have seen already, the injunctions of the holiness code are not designed to safeguard 'marriage and the family' but rather to preserve the system of male domination and the subordination of women;

(4) The injunctions of Leviticus do not cover all sexual acts but only male-male anal penetration because the targeted sin is not homosexuality but males acting as females;

(5) Much as the authors of Issues would like him to, God singularly fails to show up angry and wrathful in the face of a multitude of divergent sexual and domestic relationships reported in the Old and New Testaments which offend against the assumed normality of 'marriage and the family';

(6) The authors of Issues ignore the millions of people who are

intersexed, 1 in 50 of the human population. In over 300 pages there is not a single mention of them, and yet their existence as God's children seriously undermines the ideology the Issues authors are passing off as 'God's plan'.

The authors of Issues briefly raise the question of why the Old Testament is silent about lesbianism. They admit openly that they do not know, and treat that as though it were not a problem for them. It is a huge problem for them. It very strongly suggests that they are indeed barking up the wrong tree and that the God of the Jews did not condemn homosexuality at all. The fact that they sweep this under the carpet with a couple of cursory comments amounts to a further example of textual abuse, in the sense that they are happy to condemn lesbians on the basis of not just meagre evidence but no evidence at all.

(3c) Anglicans and St Paul

You will not be surprised to hear that the same kind of textual abuse continues in the Issues discussion of Paul's letters. We need to remember that in Paul's time there was no real concept of a homosexual orientation and it is virtually certain therefore that he assumed wrongly that everybody is naturally heterosexual.

Paul's words in the letter to the Romans seem therefore to imply that this behaviour arises not so much from a *disoriented desire* as from an *inordinate desire*. It was a common belief in the Ancient world that homosexuality arose from the same carnal desire as heterosexuality. As Victor Furnish (1979) puts it, the ancient moralists considered homosexual behaviour to be 'the most extreme expression of heterosexual lust'. The early Church Father, John Chrysostom, wrote 'you will see that all such desire stems from a greed which will not remain within its usual bounds.'

As we know, what Paul was concerned with was idolatry and homosexuality as one of the punishments for it, God giving people over to this inordinate desire which made them lust after others of the same sex. The authors of Issues quote approvingly the words of CK Barrett: *In the obscene pleasures to which Paul refers is to be seen precisely that perversion of the created order which may be expected when men put the creation in place of the Creator. That idolatry has such consequences is to Paul a plain mark of God's wrath.*

They go on to cite at length several other commentators who argue for the same brutal and inhuman interpretation. All semblance of a balanced discussion exits at this point. Nowhere do they consider the obvious problems with this view discussed earlier:

(1) Paul's actual words do not treat homosexuality as a sin but as a shameful social embarrassment;

(2) It is perfectly obvious that people do not commit idolatry first and then get made homosexual by God;

(3) There are many people whose lives are full of what Issues would see as idolatry who are not homosexual;

(4) There are many non-idolatrous homosexuals who lead pure and holy lives dedicated to Christ and yet remain homosexual;

(5) The epidemiology of homosexuality seems to be fairly constant across all societies and is unrelated to idolatry.

One of the more notorious commentators quoted in Issues is Robert Gagnon. He writes about the obviousness of homosexuality being 'contrary to nature' because the penis and the vagina fit so well together. Just in case you do not fully grasp his meaning he helpfully and tastefully elucidates further: *Neither the anus, the orifice for excreting waste products, nor the mouth, the orifice for taking in food, are complementary orifices for the male member.*

This gross view reduces people to mere biology. It reveals an abysmal lack of understanding of human relationships. Not only does it neglect the emotional dimension of human life, it is ludicrously wrong even in its own limited terms. It seems unaware that all these bodily organs are erogenous zones capable of pleasurable stimulation. Gagnon feigns not to know that heterosexuals regularly indulge in oral and anal sex as part of their love making, not to mention kissing. What is that in Gagnon's terms if not the illicit use of two orifices rubbed together for sensual pleasure! It does not reflect well on the authors of Issues that they rely on this dubious expert so uncritically.

The authors of Issues take a similarly cavalier approach to Paul's letter to the Corinthians, chapter 6, where as we have seen, the major problem is the meaning of the Greek words 'malakoi' and 'arsenokoitai'. They quote approvingly six scholars who support the nineteenth and twentieth century interpretation of these words to implicate gay people rather than male prostitutes. They then quote three scholars who believe these words have got nothing to do with same sex love, but only in order to criticise their ideas.

And despite all the acknowledged uncertainty amongst Biblical scholars the authors of Issues still unequivocally declare that: *These (words) have traditionally been seen as practising homosexuals, and understanding the text in this way has led to its being seen as clearly condemning homosexual behaviour as contrary to the law of God and as a bar to inheriting God's Kingdom.* (p 137).

Saying these terms have 'traditionally been seen as practising homosexuals' is really a disingenuous use of language. As we have seen in chapter D5, the word 'homosexual' is a nineteenth century invention so it can hardly be said to be steeped in two millennia of tradition.

And then, since it seems pretty clear that this is about some kind of exploitative prostitution, it is a basic category mistake to claim it as a condemnation of same sex love. To make this point utterly transparent, Stephen Bates (2004) bids us compare the phrase 'practising homosexuals' with the phrase 'practising heterosexuals'. Having sex with prostitutes is something 'practising heterosexuals' do. So is love-making within marriage. Are we to condemn love-making within marriage because some heterosexual men pay for sex with prostitutes? Clearly this is nonsense.

On the basis of this doubtful interpretation of Paul's letters in Issues, the Lambeth Conference in 1998, in the famous, some might say notorious, Resolution 1.10, which as we have already noted has come to take on the aura of magisterial teaching in a church without a magisterium, 'rejects homosexual practice as incompatible with Scripture'. And from this point it goes on to declare that 'abstinence is right for those who are not called to marriage'.

To this grim message, I believe Issues adds a further hypocrisy. It condemns the 'irrational fear of homosexuals' but ignores its own role in creating 'irrational fear' through its negative and irrational teaching based on an abusive use of the text.

From defence to affirmation

And here endeth the lessons of the Defensive Testament. The single overriding lesson is that the Bible does not condemn same sex love. All of the summary sheets in the preceding six chapters are designed to equip LGBT people with self-defence arguments to protect themselves not against the Bible but against the leaders of the patriarchal churches. These Christian leaders engage in Biblical casuistry to defend essentially ideological positions which deny LGBT people equal human rights. These Christian leaders also do their level best to suppress and enforce silence about parts of the Bible where LGBT lives, identities and relationships are celebrated. It is to these that we now turn in the Affirmative Testament. www.thegaygospels.com

LGBT Self defence
Summary Sheet D7: Textual abuse

1. Textual abuse is a selective interpretation of an isolated text to give it a decontextualised, prejudicial contemporary meaning.

2. In Catholic teaching: homosexuality is an objective disorder tending towards an intrinsic moral evil.

3. In Evangelical teaching: dispassionate exegesis supports the longstanding prohibition on homosexuality.

4. In Anglican teaching: homosexual practice is incompatible with scripture.

5. Distortions of Sodom:
   (i) miss out the first chapter so that the point of the story is missed
   (ii) gang rape is equated with homosexual love
   (iii) ignore the fact that God destroys Sodom because of inhospitality not homosexuality
   (iv) ignore the fact that Lot only refers to hospitality
   (v) ignore Lot's incest with his own daughters

6. Distortions of Leviticus:
   (i) ignore the fact that Leviticus is only against male anal intercourse
   (ii) ignore the fact that Leviticus is only against men behaving as women
   (iii) there is no basis for picking out the male-male sex proscription while ignoring others
   (iv) there is no basis for ignoring the death penalty prescriptions
   (v) ignore the New Testament overriding of the Holiness code

7. Distortions of St Paul:
   (i) ignore the fact that St Paul thought homosexuality the

punishment for idolatry

(ii) ignore the fact that St Paul thought homosexuality shameful, not sinful

(iii) ignore the fact that St Paul thought many other things more important

8. After Jesus everything is to be assessed against twin 'love commandments' – God and neighbour. Anti-LGBT teachings fail dismally against these criteria.

The Affirmative Testament Chapter A1

Jesus and the Beloved Disciple

From his words and deeds we know that Jesus loved all his disciples.

However the Gospel of John tells us of one disciple that Jesus loved in some very particular way.

This disciple is present beside Jesus during all the most critical episodes in his passion, death and resurrection, and he is the only disciple of whom this is true. He is never named but is always referred to as 'the disciple whom Jesus loved'. His special relationship with Jesus is evident in the gospel accounts of:

the Last Supper
the Crucifixion
the empty tomb
the resurrection appearance on the shore
the foundation of the church in the commissioning of Peter

The singling out of this one disciple, who has no particular role in Jesus' mission, and who is only ever described in terms of his being 'beloved', makes clear that what is going on here is some kind of relationship which goes beyond the love that Jesus felt for the other disciples.

(I) The Last Supper

Jesus is in Jerusalem with his disciples for the feast of the Passover. During this fateful final meal he announces that one of them will betray him. They all look perplexed. Peter wants to know who it is. But instead of asking Jesus directly he asks the disciple whom Jesus loved. The Beloved Disciple is positioned remarkably close beside Jesus: *Now there was leaning on Jesus' bosom one of his disciples, whom Jesus loved. Simon Peter therefore beckoned to him, that he should ask who it should be of whom he spake. He then lying on Jesus' breast saith uno him, Lord, who is it? Jesus answered, He it is, to whom I shall give a sop, when I have dipped it. And when he had dipped the sop he gave it to Judas Iscariot, the son of Simon.* John 13:21-26.

In ancient times the normal posture for friends dining together was often lying on mats or pillows. But it would nevertheless be unusual for two males to be cuddled up together in such physical closeness and bodily intimacy. And yet Peter and the other disciples appear untroubled by it.

In fact not only does Peter seem untroubled by it, he appears to recognise the special quality of the relationship by asking the Beloved Disciple as an appropriate means to put a question to Jesus. At modern day dinner parties it is not uncommon for people to ask the wife what the husband thinks. It is simply an acknowledgement of the reality of a relationship which transcends the two partners as individuals. It is difficult to see what other sense can be made of Peter's not simply asking Jesus himself.

What are we to make of this? There is an intimacy here which goes beyond the friendship and love which characterises Jesus' relationship to all other members of his group. If we are to follow the plain sense of the text it looks as if Jesus had a same sex lover.

(2) The Crucifixion

We meet the Beloved Disciple again at the foot of the cross during the crucifixion. He is the only disciple there. The others, including Peter, have run away. The disciples had all deserted Jesus because they believed that with his execution as a common criminal the game was up, the mission had ended in failure, and now their lives were in danger as known associates of a convicted troublemaker. So why did the Beloved Disciple not go with them?

Why did he stay and risk his own life to be with Jesus? Jesus' words as he is dying suggest the reason: *But there stood by the cross of Jesus, his mother, the sister of his mother, Mary the wife of Clopas, and Mary the Magdalene. Jesus, seeing his mother and the disciple standing by whom he loved, he said to his mother 'Woman, behold your son'. Then he says to the disciple, 'behold your mother'! And from that hour the disciple took her to his own.* John 19 :25-27.

This text is hugely significant. Jesus is dying. If he had had a heterosexual relationship with Mary Magdalene, as many people such as Dan Brown have argued, it would have been perfectly normal for him to have told his mother to look after her as the daughter-in-law she would effectively be. As so often happens, the mother of the dead son and the wife of the dead husband would take care of one another in their mutual grief.

But Jesus does not mention Mary Magdalene, despite the fact that she is standing there in front of him. He says nothing to her. Instead, as Jennings (2003) notes, he explicitly puts the man he loved in 'an adoptive relationship' with his mother. What conclusion can we draw from this other than that this disciple whom Jesus loved is, in modern terminology, his significant other? His mother and the Beloved Disciple are the two most important human relationships in Jesus' life as it ebbs away.

Note also that Jesus' first concern is for the beloved rather than for his mother. He tells his mother to care for this disciple as a son (in-law). We know Jesus had brothers. His concern here is therefore not for Mary. She has other sons to care for her. She is being asked to take on another, for his benefit rather than hers.

This also confirms that the special relationship between Jesus and the disciple whom he loved was open and acknowledged, rather than clandestine and hidden.

(3) The empty tomb

The Beloved Disciple appears next in the story of the empty tomb. Mary Magdalene goes to the tomb and finds the stone has been moved and Jesus' body has disappeared. She looks for Peter, the leader of Jesus' disciples, to tell him. She also seeks out the Beloved Disciple. The gospel text does not tell us why but it seems reasonable to assume that she sees these two as the most important; Peter, because he is the leader, and the Beloved Disciple because of his special relationship with Jesus. Here then is further evidence of another key player in the story taking account of the significance of this relationship.

They immediately run to the tomb. The Beloved Disciple gets there first, but then waits for Peter to arrive before going in. This may be because Peter is regarded as the strongest and boldest. But also the Beloved Disciple might well still be traumatized by having witnessed Jesus' cruel death, and therefore horrified at the idea of having to see the damaged and disfigured corpse of his lover.

However, he does muster up the courage to go in, after Peter has established that there is no body in there. When the Beloved Disciple sees the discarded sheets and the handkerchief which had been on Jesus' head: *He saw and believed; for as yet they did not know the writing, that he must rise from the dead.* John 20:10.

The Beloved Disciple is thus the first disciple, the very first person, to believe in Christ's resurrection. The fact that the Gospel states this is of great significance because it might have been expected that Peter, the future first pope, would be the first believer. Or Mary Magdalene, if she was supposed to be Jesus' straight lover. Either of these might have been more 'convenient' for the Church which would eventually emerge. But it is neither of them: it is the disciple whom Jesus loved.

(4) The resurrection appearance on the shore

Subsequently there are a number of resurrection appearances. One of the best known is when Peter and a number of the disciples go night fishing but catch nothing. In the morning they encounter a stranger on the shore who instructs them where to put the nets, which immediately fill to overflowing with fish. Again, it is the Beloved Disciple who first recognises Jesus: *Therefore that disciple whom Jesus loved saith unto Peter 'it is the Lord'.* John 21: 7.

Here again it might have been expected that Peter would be the first to realise that the stranger on the shore is Jesus. He is the leader, the strongest, he will become the rock on which Christ's church will be built. But he does not recognise his Lord. It is the Beloved Disciple who may well have perceived the presence of his beloved in the kinds of intangible intimate familiarities which characterise partnerships based on close emotional attachment. So once more Peter relies on the Beloved Disciple to know what is happening. This fact underlines the importance of the Beloved Disciple's special intimacy with Jesus, even beyond death.

(5) The foundation of the Church in the commissioning of Peter

They return to the beach and fry the fish for breakfast. Afterwards the resurrected Jesus asks Peter three times if he loves him and he commands Peter to 'feed my sheep'. This is a moment of vital significance in the whole Christian story. Jesus' interrogation of Peter's love for him, and his commissioning of Peter as shepherd of Christ's flock, is understood by the Catholic hierarchy and others to constitute the establishment of the church with Peter as universal pastor, effectively the first pope. In the absence of Jesus' bodily presence in the world, it is Peter who will become Christ's 'vicar on earth'. Peter clearly understands this and yet he still asks Jesus whether this includes the Beloved Disciple: *Turning, Peter sees the disciple that Jesus loved following them, who was also the one who leaned on Jesus' chest at the supper............ Peter seeing this one says to Jesus, 'Lord and what of him?' Jesus says to him, 'if I want him to remain until I come, what is that to you? You follow me!'* John 21:20-24.

Peter's question about the Beloved Disciple is most odd. Here is Peter beginning the task Jesus has set for him of caring for all his followers. Why would he even raise the question of whether he is also to care for the Beloved Disciple? Why does he not take it for granted that the Beloved Disciple is simply one of the flock he is now responsible for?

The answer is obvious. Peter has clearly come to regard the Beloved Disciple as much more than just a disciple, much more than just a human soul, much more than just one of the sheep. And astonishingly, Jesus confirms the truth of this. He declares himself responsible for the beloved's fate, once again distinguishing this man from all others now entrusted to Peter's care.

The other disciples take this to mean that Jesus will protect the Beloved Disciple from harm until his return. They are wrong about this but that is not the point. What matters is that they think that this relationship is so close as to make the idea credible. The Gospel of John tells us: *Then went this saying abroad among the brethren, that this disciple should not die: yet Jesus said not unto him, he shall not die; but if I will that he tarry till I come, what is that to thee?* John 21:23.

This assumption speaks volumes about how the special relationship appeared to them. Clearly they believe that Jesus had promised the Beloved Disciple that he would not die. And they believed this in the full knowledge that Jesus would not prevent their deaths. In the same passage Jesus specifically tells Peter he will die by crucifixion: *When thou wast young, thou girdest thyself, and walkedst whither thou wouldest: but when thou shalt be old, thou shalt stretch forth thy hands, and another shall gird thee, and carry thee whither thou wouldest not. This spake he, signifying by what manner of death he should glorify God.* John 21:18-19.

So why do they think this particular disciple will be protected from death? They must be conscious of some huge difference separating him off from even the greatest of the disciples, Peter. It is clear that it is not because of any particular virtue or spiritual superiority, for nothing is ever said about this disciple except that

Jesus loved him. It appears this love was so self-evident to the disciple group that they found the idea of Jesus saving him from death perfectly understandable and unexceptional.

A homoerotic bond

What exactly was the nature of this relationship? Clearly it was a very close emotional bond. But taken together, all the pieces of evidence in John's Gospel suggest it was also a mutual homoerotic attraction based on reciprocal desire and delight.

At the Last Supper we have a picture of real affection involving bodily intimacy, which is seen, recognised and approved by the other disciples. It is very telling that Peter assumes that if Jesus has told anyone who the traitor is, it will be the Beloved Disciple. Jesus' concern on the cross for this man mirrors exactly the concern of any dying lover for the future welfare of the beloved. He wants him taken care of and instructs his mother accordingly. Neither here nor anywhere does Jesus express love for his mother. He simply wants her to look after the Beloved Disciple. Moreover, neither Mary nor the other women present appear at all surprised. Like Peter they seem to take this relationship for granted. At the empty tomb, the Beloved Disciple's behaviour is what you would expect from a lover in such traumatic circumstances. He has recently witnessed the cruel torturing to death of his partner, and he can hardly bear now to contemplate seeing the body. And then only the Beloved Disciple senses that the stranger on the shore is the risen Christ, as if the love that he shared with Jesus has endured through to the new life. Later Jesus seems to endorse this intuition. His concern for the Beloved Disciple is presented as eternal, literally undying. This man is to be the one and only human soul to be put beyond Petrine care and to be tended directly by the Son of God. Could there be a more powerful expression of love?

To all intents and purposes what we have here in John's Gospel looks like a real love story. It would be perfectly natural for such an intensely loving relationship to encompass physical erotic activity, although of course the Biblical text does not describe any such acts. But then neither does it in the case of relationships which we know were sexual, so this means nothing.

One other point is important. Recall that Jesus asks Peter three times if he loves him. It has been suggested that this has the effect of 'undoing' the three times Peter denied Jesus previously. But it also emphasises the importance of Peter's loving Jesus. In the case of the Beloved Disciple, however, the emphasis is always on love in the other direction. It is always about Jesus loving the Beloved Disciple. One possible reading of this evidence is that Jesus' fundamental erotic orientation is towards this same-sex lover. He is the 'driver', the dominant partner, in the relationship.

Jesus wants Peter to declare his love for him so that he can be sure he can rely on him to carry out his important mission. By contrast Jesus does not want or expect anything from the Beloved Disciple. We do not read that Jesus asked the Beloved disciple to declare his love. Jesus just loves him and he expresses his love unconditionally in the scenes recounted above.

This reading of the text also explains why Peter and the Beloved Disciple get on so well together. They both find joy in their relationship with Jesus but in quite different ways. Peter has an important job to do for Jesus. The Beloved Disciple has no distinctive role or responsibility. Peter does not want to be Jesus' lover. And the Beloved Disciple does not want to be leader. They are no threat to each other.

Consequently Peter is happy to acknowledge the special place of the Beloved Disciple, who equally is presumably happy to acknowledge Peter's leadership role. This mutuality contrasts starkly with Peter's later relationship with the apostle Paul, who was in many senses a rival leader, and with whom there were some stormy exchanges.

If it were not for two thousand years of Church inspired erotophobia in general and homophobia in particular, it would surely be blindingly obvious to everyone reading St John's Gospel that the relationship between Jesus and the Beloved Disciple was homoerotic in character. True, these episodes are separated in the text, and it is only when they are all put together that the accumulated evidence appears overwhelming.

But this juxtaposition is not difficult to do, it is just that the Church has not wanted to do it. At the very least the story of the Beloved Disciple raises serious questions about Jesus' sexual orientation, and it is this issue which forms the subject of the next chapter.

LGBT Self affirmation
Summary Sheet A1: Jesus and The
Beloved Disciple

1. St John's Gospel speaks of one disciple 'whom Jesus loved' in a manner different from his love for all the other disciples.

2. This disciple is present at the crucial events of Jesus' passion, death and resurrection.

3. **At the Last Supper** there is physical closeness and intimacy recognised and accepted by Peter and the other disciples.

4. **At the Crucifixion** the Beloved Disciple is the only disciple to remain after all the others have run away. As he is dying, Jesus puts him in an adoptive relationship with Mary, his mother. He says nothing to Mary Magdalene.

5. **At the empty tomb** the Beloved Disciple arrives before Peter but cannot go in. When he does and sees the empty sheets he is the first to believe.

6. **At the resurrection appearance** on the shore, it is the Beloved Disciple, not Peter, the leader of the disciples, who recognises the risen Jesus.

7. **At the foundation of the church** when Jesus commissions Peter as the future shepherd of all his flock, the Beloved Disciple is put outside of Petrine care, to be looked after directly by Jesus.

8. Taken together these scenes depict a close homoerotic and emotional bond between Jesus and the Beloved Disciple, recognisable in terms which would today be described as a gay relationship, chaste or otherwise.

The Affirmative Testament Chapter A2

Jesus' Sexual Orientation

Although it is not much talked about, there has been a long tradition of interpreting the passages in the Gospel of John about the Beloved disciple to mean that Jesus was gay, having a basically homosexual orientation.

St Aelred (12th century)

In the twelfth century the English abbot of Rievaulx, St Aelred, whose feast day is celebrated by the Catholic Church every year on 12th January, regarded love between males as a natural and beautiful phenomenon. In a much quoted passage, which has become the manifesto of a number of gay organisations, Aelred describes movingly the joy of being in love with another man: *It is no small consolation in this life to have someone you can unite with you in intimate affection and the embrace of a holy love, someone in whom your spirit can rest, to whom you can pour out your soul, to whose pleasant exchanges, as to soothing songs, you can fly in sorrow.....with whose spiritual kisses, as with remedial salves, you may draw out all the weariness of your restless anxieties,. A man who can shed tears with you in your worries, be happy with you when things go well, search out with you the answers to your problems, whom with the ties of charity you can lead into the depths of your heart;....where the sweetness of the spirit flows between you, where you so join yourself and cleave to him that soul mingles with soul and two become one.*

This is an inspiring hymn to same sex affection and for LGBT people it has great significance. The use of the words 'cleave to' and 'two become one' appear to be a direct reference to the Genesis text discussed earlier in the chapter about the so-called creation ordinances: *Therefore shall a man leave his father and his mother, and shall cleave unto his wife: and they shall be one flesh* Genesis 2:24.

By using this language Aelred seems to be deliberately putting the relationship here between two men on a par with the husband-wife relationship pictured in Genesis. The clear implication is that it is an acceptable alternative for those to whom such same sex attraction comes naturally, arguably as part of God's intended creation. In defence of his position Aelred does not just turn to the terminology of Genesis, but draws also very specifically on the example of Jesus and the Beloved Disciple.

And lest this sort of sacred love should seem improper to anyone, Jesus himself, in everything like us, patient and compassionate with us in every matter, transfigured it through the expression of his own love; for he allowed one, not all, to recline on his breast as a sign of his special love. Quoted in Jennings (2003) p 76.

This is quite an astonishing text coming as it does, not from any kind of homosexual apologist or gay activist, but from an actual canonised saint of the Catholic Church. Of course the Church authorities now try to argue that the language is all symbolic and Aelred was not really gay. But the words speak for themselves. Gay people everywhere will find resonances of their own experience in these phrases of delight and endearment. Aelred wrote a great deal about same sex friendship and encouraged it between the monks for whom he was responsible. In his celebrated treatise 'On Spiritual Friendship' he developed a theology of friendship based on equality which has subsequently been applied to male-female relationships. Here once again then we meet Jesus modelling relationships of mutual care and love, twelve centuries on, through this great medieval saint's interpretation of the story of Christ's love for the Beloved Disciple.

Christopher Marlowe (16th century)

Christopher Marlowe was a great English playwright born in

Canterbury in 1564, the same year as William Shakespeare. In his brief life he wrote several acclaimed dramas including the *Tragical History of Doctor Faustus* and *Edward II*. In 1593 he was killed in a drunken brawl in a tavern in Deptford. At least this is the accepted version. There are suspicions that his murder was actually a good deal more complex and murkier. At the inquest held into his death, one of those accused of his murder, Richard Baines, claimed that he deserved to die because he had constantly blasphemed about Jesus and the Beloved Disciple, saying that: *St John the Evangelist was bedfellow to Christ and leaned always in his bosom, that he used him as the sinners of Sodoma.*

Baines also reported that Marlowe thought: *That all they that love not Tobacco and Boies were fooles.*

It looks like we have here an Elizabethan gay man perceiving the gay sensitivities evident in St John's gospel, and discussing them with others who clearly understood what he was talking about.

King James 1st (17th century)

From an early age the future King James 1st showed a marked proclivity towards males. His great lover was George Villiers, the Duke of Buckingham who rose to this aristocratic position from being a cupbearer thanks to his relationship with the King. James commissioned the bible we now know as the King James' Version and obviously read it assiduously, explicitly using the story of Jesus and the Beloved Disciple to justify his relationship with his own lover: *I love the Earl of Buckingham more than anyone else, and more than you who are here assembled......Jesus Christ did the same and therefore I cannot be blamed. Christ had his John, and I have my George.*

Jeremy Bentham (18th century)

Bentham was a highly influential political philosopher associated particularly with the idea of utilitarianism and the search for 'the greatest good for the greatest number of people'. This shaped his ideas about homosexuality, and he was deeply opposed to the criminalisation of gay sex which he viewed as a victimless crime. At the time the penalty for buggery was public hanging. He was horrified by the brutality and hatred shown to homosexuals. He complains that *in England nothing less than the heart's blood of the victims marked out for slaughter* can appease popular loathing, and he describes the face of a judge who has just sentenced two men to hang as *'glistening with delight and exultation'*. In this climate he was fearful of the consequences for himself if people knew of his opinions, and his papers on the subject were not published in his lifetime. It was not until 1985 that Louis Crompton published some of Bentham's writings in the book *'Byron and Greek Love: Homophobia in Nineteenth-Century England'*. Amongst these was Bentham's work entitled *'Not Paul but Jesus'* in which he analyses the Biblical texts relating to homosexuality and concludes that it was Paul who was responsible for Christianity's hatred of homosexuals. In Jesus by contrast Bentham finds someone with a homoerotic sensitivity.

He argues very simply and very logically that it is difficult to see what the author of St John's Gospel could possibly have had in mind in describing *'in so pointed a manner accompanied by such circumstances of fondness'* Jesus' love for the Beloved Disciple if it was not a homosexual relationship. It is quite clear that this love is of a different order from that Jesus felt for the other disciples. Bentham is perplexed by the fact that the Beloved Disciple has no other function in the narrative than to be Jesus' beloved. He is not given any special role, he is not said to be particularly good at preaching, he serves no identifiable purpose in Jesus' mission: *For of this nothing is to be found in Saint John by which he can stand in comparison with Saint Peter, and on no occasion is the rough fisherman to be seen 'leaning in the bosom of Jesus' or 'lying on his breast'* (Crompton p 278,279).

So the affectionate intimacy Jesus shows towards the Beloved

Disciple looks like pure love and is in no sense understandable as mere closeness between two men engaged on the same project. The coarse Peter who clearly is central to the mission gets no such treatment from Jesus.

Groddeck and Psychoanalysis (19th/20th century)

In his discussion of the references across the centuries to Jesus and the Beloved Disciple as lovers Jennings (2003) highlights the significance of the psychoanalytic ideas of Georg Walther Groddeck who has an interesting take on homosexuality in general. For him it is primary, especially for females. Our initial erotic attachment is to the self and then is quickly transferred to the mother. In the case of girls this is homosexual in nature. What needs to be explained he thinks is not why there are homosexuals but how people possibly become heterosexual. He feels that Western civilisation must be: *...at least surprised at that curious phrase in the Gospel concerning Christ's disciple, 'whom Jesus loved', and who lay upon the Lord's breast. We make nothing of it at all. To all this evidence we are blind. We are not to see what is there to be seen.*

In the first place, the Church forbids it. Obviously she derives this prohibition from the Old Testament, the whole spirit of which was directed to bringing all sexual activity into direct association with the begetting of children, and, as a result of priestly ambition, she purposely made this inherited human instinct into a sin in order to lord it over the stricken conscience. This was particularly opportune for the Christian Church since it was able to deal with the root Hellenic culture in its execration of male love. Groddeck (1949) ps 263-264.

Bentham was writing in the context of a legal examination of the text and came to the conclusion that the homoerotic nature of Jesus relationship with the Beloved Disciple is plainly visible before our eyes. And now here too, in the context of a psychoanalytic theory about the primacy of homosexuality, Groddeck is saying 'just look at the text and see what is obviously there'. He urges us to take off the blinkers which the churches have put on us and which distort what we see. We just need to look honestly and dispassionately at what is blindingly self-evident.

There is a sense in which both Bentham and Groddick are like the little boy in Hans Christian Anderson's story of the 'Emperor's New Clothes' who points to the obvious truth that the Emperor is naked. The heterosexual clothes that the Church has put on Jesus' sexuality are entirely imaginary.

Bishop Hugh Montefiore (20th century)

Somebody who shouted even louder that the Emperor is naked was Canon Hugh Montefiore. In 1967 he gave a talk to a public meeting in Oxford, the text of which was published a year later. It caused outrage at the time but clearly did not impede his career in the Church of England, as he later became the Bishop of Birmingham. In this famous talk he raised the question of why Jesus was not married: *Men usually remain unmarried for three reasons: either because they cannot afford to marry or there are no girls to marry (neither of these factors need have deterred Jesus); or because it is inexpedient to marry in light of their vocation (we have already ruled this out during the 'hidden years' of Jesus' life); or because they are homosexual in nature, in as much as women hold no special attraction for them. This homosexual explanation is one which we must not ignore. According to the gospels, women were his friends but it is men whom he is said to love. Possibly the hearer may shrink from this idea in disgust. If so let him consider that these are the very same emotions with which the Jews of Jesus' day received the idea that the Messiah of Judah died a criminal's death upon a Roman cross.*

What Bishop Montefiore wanted to point out is that the visceral reaction of so many people to ideas they do not want to hear says nothing about whether these ideas are actually true or not. Jews could not accept that Jesus was the Messiah because they could not believe that he would suffer the humiliation of death on a cross. Christians have no problem with this. The lesson according to Montefiore is that Christians might need to get over their revulsion at the idea that Jesus was gay and simply recognise the evidence in front of their eyes.

Elton John (20th/21st century)

During the 21st century it has become possible to talk openly about homosexuality in a way that was inconceivable in earlier times. In this cultural context the idea that Jesus might have been homosexual is openly discussed, way beyond the boundaries of just theology or religion. Famously Elton John expressed an opinion that is more widely held than ever before, that Jesus was obviously a gay man: *I think Jesus was a compassionate super-intelligent gay man who understood human problems. On the cross he forgave the people who crucified him. Jesus wanted us to be loving and forgiving. I don't know what makes people so cruel. Try being a gay woman in the Middle East- you're as good as dead.*

It is becoming now more difficult for the patriarchal churches to maintain that Jesus was somehow not sexual, did not experience desire, did not have erections and nocturnal emissions as all other men do. And yet the churches wish also to claim that Jesus was 'fully human', that he was in the words of St John's gospel, the word 'made flesh'. This position is untenable because it is self-contradictory. If Jesus was a fully human man then he was necessarily a fully sexualised being.

Sexual orientation

The question then arises as to where Jesus' sexual energy was directed. As Montefiore noted above, in none of the gospel accounts of Jesus' life do we read anything to suggest that Jesus had any erotic interest in women. Some attention has been given to his friendship with Mary Magdalene but the evidence is lacking. Only in the realms of imaginative fiction does this heterosexual fantasy assume any verisimilitude. There is, however, as we have seen considerable evidence for his interest in the Beloved Disciple. Indeed this disciple has no other function in the Johanine narrative than to be Jesus' beloved.

The Rich Young Man

Furthermore, in other gospel texts there are some other pieces of supporting evidence for the thesis that Jesus had a gay eye. Jennings (2003) points out that in the Gospel of Mark Jesus' attention is drawn toward a 'rich young man'. This man had approached to ask him what it was necessary to do in order to inherit eternal life. Jesus tells him to keep the commandments. The man replies that he always has. At this point Mark tells us:

Jesus, looking at him, loved him and said, 'you lack one thing, go, sell what you own, and give the money to the poor, and you will have treasure in heaven; then come, follow me.' When he heard this he was shocked and went away grieving, for he had many possessions. Mark10: 17-22.

Why does Mark say that Jesus 'loved him'? What can this mean? What kind of love is in play here? Jesus did not know the rich young man, so how could he love him? And Mark's use of the word 'love' is intriguing since nowhere else in his gospel does he tell us that Jesus loved anybody. This young man has clearly made an impact on him. Note also that Mark reports Jesus 'looking at him'. The Greek word *'emblepein'* suggests Jesus scrutinises his appearance carefully, in contemporary language it might be said that Jesus was 'eyeing him up', finding joy and delight in appreciating his physical beauty, and realising that his desire was becoming aroused. Taken together this 'looking' and this 'loving' are strongly suggestive of an erotic awakening that would be entirely consistent with Jesus' being 'fully human'.

The Naked Youth in the Garden

Elsewhere in Mark's gospel we meet another young man, a youth who has been alongside Jesus in the Garden of Gethsemane and who the text tells us was naked. After Jesus is arrested we read:

And they all forsook him and fled. And a youth accompanied him, clothed in a linen cloth over his nudity. And they seized him. And he, leaving the linen cloth fled nude. Mark 14:50-52.

In his discussion of this story, Jeremy Bentham argued that the Greek terminology used to describe the boy and the linen cloth indicate clearly that he was a male prostitute, which in the Hellenistic culture of the time would have been an unexceptionable commonplace. Bentham believed that there was a homoerotic incident taking place in the Garden of Gethsemane. It is certainly odd. All the disciples have run off. Jesus and the boy are both arrested, but the boy escapes by virtue of the loose clothing he is wearing. In this way he slipped literally through his captors' hands. But who was he, and what was he doing there in the first place? Adrian Thatcher (2008) suggests that: *Jesus, we may speculate, was just the sort of company with whom a sexually exploited young man could relax and feel accepted.* Thatcher (2008) p. 33.

That Mark has troubled to include this event in his gospel narrative means that he regards it as significant.

Secret Mark

There is a further text which may shed some light on this situation. This is to be found not in Mark's gospel but in a document now known as 'Secret Mark'. This is actually a letter of Clement of Alexandria written in about 200AD which was discovered only in 1958. It has been alleged that this might be either an ancient or a modern forgery (see Wikipedia for details), but these allegations have been dismissed by a number of respected academics and theologians. Many scholars believe this text to be in effect a version of Mark's gospel earlier than the one we have in the New Testament. In this version much more detail is given. Secret Mark's story starts with a woman coming to Jesus to ask him to raise her dead brother. Jesus goes to the tomb where the dead boy lies, rolls away the stone, and calls him back to life. *But the youth, looking upon him, loved him and began to beseech him that he might be with him. And going out of the tomb they came into the house of the youth, for he was rich. And after six days Jesus told him what he was to do and in the evening the youth comes to him, wearing a linen cloth over his naked body. And he remained with him that night, for Jesus taught him the mystery of the kingdom of God. And thence, arising, he returned to the other side of the Jordan.* (Quoted in Jennings 2003 p. 115)

This account recalls both the raising of Lazarus and the story of the rich young man, except that this time it is the young man who looks intently *(emblepein)* at Jesus and loves him, reciprocating the love expressed by Jesus in the standard Gospel of Mark. It is as if this version gives the full story of which Mark has only partial details. In Clement's Mark the rich young man learns from the experience of death and resurrection into the love of Jesus the meaning of inheriting eternal life. But the homoerotic elements are pronounced. The young man begs to stay with Jesus, and Jesus goes back with him to his house for a week. Going back to someone's house is a familiar experience for gay men. In this way the relationship between them is established before the arrest in the Garden of Gethsemane and this explains the steadfast loyalty of the boy in staying with Jesus in the face of danger even after the disciples have fled in panic.

The Clementine version of Mark concludes with further confirmation of the relationship between Jesus and the young man: *...and he comes into Jericho, and the sister of the youth whom Jesus loved and his mother and Salome were there, and Jesus did not receive them.*

As Jennings (2003) points out, Clement's letter refers not only to this earlier version of Mark's gospel but also to yet another version, which we do not have, in which the idea of a sexual relationship between Jesus and the youth is made even more explicit. This version is associated with the Carpocratians, a group vilified for their sexual licence by Clement, who was virulently anti-gay and responsible for introducing strong elements of erotophobia and homophobia into Christianity. He is highly critical of the Carpocratians whom he condemns mercilessly for their concern with carnal pleasure. The point for our present discussion is not Clement's views, but the access that he inadvertently gives us into versions of the gospel texts which were circulating in his time which appear to leave no room for doubt concerning Jesus' involvement in homosexual relations.

Jesus' gayness

In all these documents it is clear that there is much uncertainty surrounding the identity of the rich young man, the naked youth in the Garden of Gethsemane, the Beloved Disciple, and indeed also Lazarus, 'whom Jesus loved' and also raised from the dead (John 11:1-26). Some Biblical scholars believe they are all the same man (see for example Robert Williams, reported in Goss (1993) p214 note 59). Others think more than one man is implicated. For our present purposes the identity issues are of secondary importance. What matters is that we have before our eyes extensive material evidence, much of it sanctified as divinely inspired gospel text, that Jesus' sexuality was predominantly, possibly exclusively, male focused.

Two thousand years of tradition based on heterosexist ideology have sought to suppress these facts. Clement's letter makes clear that there were earlier versions of Mark's gospel which reported openly on Jesus' gayness. Gradually these versions were denounced by authority figures such as Clement and homophobic prohibitions were introduced into the Church. Over time the publicly accepted version of Mark is left with only tiny homoerotic fragments. Only in the Gospel of John with the story of the Beloved Disciple do we still have a substantial narrative implying that Jesus was homoerotically inclined. However, the uncovering and reassembling of all the pieces of textual evidence which the Christian tradition has sought to keep

LGBT Self affirmation
Summary Sheet A2: Jesus' Sexual Orientation

1. There is a long but little known tradition of understanding Jesus' relationship with the Beloved Disciple as essentially homosexual in nature, albeit possibly chaste.

2. In the 12th century St Aelred wrote of Jesus 'special love' and built a whole theology of same sex friendship on it.

3. In the 16th century Christopher Marlowe, noted Elizabethan playwright, believed the Beloved Disciple to be 'bedfellow to Christ' and their relationship to be explicitly sexual.

4. In the 17th century King James 1st of England used the story of the Beloved Disciple to justify his own explicitly homosexual relationship with the Duke of Buckingham.

5. In the 18th century the political philosopher Jeremy Bentham interpreted Jesus' relationship with the Beloved Disciple as a love affair; love of a quite different order from that which Jesus showed to the other apostles.

6. In the 20th century Canon Hugh Montefiore argued that Jesus' being homosexual is the best explanation for his not getting married and for the gospel passages describing his relationship with the Beloved Disciple.

7. In the 21st century Biblical scholars weighing all the evidence suggest that 'the simplest explanation for the presence of the beloved in this narrative is the obvious one. He and Jesus were lovers.' (Jennings (2003) p 74).

8. The patriarchal Christian churches try to paint Jesus as somehow not sexual, while at the same time claiming he was 'fully human'. This is a logical impossibility and self-contradictory.

9. Further evidence that Jesus' sexual orientation was homosexual comes from the Gospel of Mark in the stories of

the rich young man and the naked youth in the Garden of Gethsemane.

10. Evidence from the letter of Clement found in 1958 shows that earlier versions of the Gospel of Mark contain explicit details of sexual relationship between Jesus and these male characters.

The Affirmative Testament Chapter A3

Jesus meets a gay couple

You were probably never told in Sunday school that Jesus had an encounter with a gay man. You may though have been told about Jesus healing the Centurion's servant. Recent biblical and linguistic research appears to show now you should have been told that the servant Jesus healed was in fact the Centurion's male lover. What your Sunday school teacher should have told you is that this story actually recounts what happened when Jesus met a gay couple.

What happened?
The story is reported in two places in the New Testament, Matthew (8: 5-13) and in Luke (7:1-10).

In Matthew's account, Jesus enters Capernaum and a centurion comes up to him. This in itself is pretty remarkable since the centurion was a Roman, and a powerful Roman at that, a key player in the forces brutally occupying the Jews' homeland. He is used to being in command. Centurions stood between the common soldier and the higher ranking officers. They were so called because they were in command of a 'century' of approximately a hundred soldiers, but some were in command of many more, up to a thousand men. The centurion himself explains how much authority he has: *For I am a man under authority, having soldiers under me: and I say to this man , 'go', and he goeth; and to another, 'come', and he cometh; and to my servant, 'do this', and he doeth it.* Matthew 8:9.

So begging help from an itinerant Jewish preacher is not exactly in character. Nevertheless the centurion says to Jesus: *'Lord, my servant is lying at home paralyzed, suffering dreadfully.'*

Jesus promises immediately to come and cure him. But the centurion says:

Lord, I am not worthy to have you under my roof; only say the word and my servant will be healed.

Jesus is amazed at the centurion's faith. He even goes so far as to say that he had not found amongst his own people anyone in Israel with such faith. He replies: *You may go; as you have believed, let it be done for you.*

Matthew tells us that 'at that very hour the servant was healed'.

Luke's version of the story is slightly different but has all the essential details contained in the Gospel of Matthew. In this retelling the centurion cannot bear to leave his dearly loved sick boy servant who is near death and so instead he sends the Elders of the Jews to plead with Jesus on his behalf to effect a cure. The Elders tell Jesus that the centurion, although a Gentile and a Roman, is a good man who loves Israel and has built a synagogue for them. Jesus agrees to go to the centurion's house with the Elders. But before they arrive the Centurion sends friends out to stop him, with the same message: *Lord trouble not thyself: for I am not worthy that thou shouldst enter under my roof: wherefore neither thought I myself worthy to come unto thee: but say in a word, and my servant shall be healed.* Luke 7: 6-7.

This statement displays an astonishing degree of humility on the part of so authoritative a figure. It also reveals a personal faith in Jesus of extraordinary depth and commitment. And here in Luke's account also Jesus declares he has never found so great a faith in anyone before, even amongst his own people in Israel. Luke's account ends with the Elders returning to the centurion's house where they 'found the servant whole that had been sick'.

How do we know the Centurion and his servant were gay?

The centurion uses two different Greek words when he speaks of his servants. The word he uses in general is *doulos* meaning servant or slave. In Matthew's account when he speaks of the one who is sick he uses the word *pais*. This word means boy and can also mean slave, servant or even son. It normally refers to someone young and only by way of either endearment or conde-scension to an adult. It could also be used for the boy slaves who were kept for sexual purposes, a practice not only common but one also regarded as normal amongst Romans. It cannot be his son because in Luke's account only the word *doulos* is used. However, the word 'boy' can also be used for an adult who is socially inferior. This was still common in the case of fully grown adult black males in the Southern United States and South Africa up to the 20th century.

However, Luke also reveals the kind of relationship the centurion has with the boy. He tells us that the boy was very *'entimos'* to the centurion. This implies that the boy was very dear to the centurion, that there was a really close emotional bond between them.

It is possible that the centurion was just a good man and upset by the impending death of a slave boy. This is unlikely however. The harsh truth is that slaves died all the time and were easily replaced by a man with as much wealth as the centurion had.

It is difficult to see what could possibly have driven a Roman centurion to be so concerned about a slave. And we know right from the outset of the story that the centurion is very concerned indeed. He does not just 'ask' Jesus to cure the boy, he begs him. In the King James Bible he 'beseeches' him. The Greek word used here is *'parakaloon'* and from its use in other Biblical texts we can be certain that it betokens a real desperation on the part of the centurion, exactly the kind of desperation that anybody watching life painfully flowing out of a lover would feel. The most probable answer is that the boy was a sexual slave but the centurion had grown very fond of him.

This was to all intents and purposes a same sex loving relationship. It might have started in the exploitation of a slave but had apparently grown into a reciprocal partnership of love, care and concern. It may well be that the centurion was actually gay, in the sense of having a fixed sexual orientation which meant he would fall in love with males rather than females.

Did Jesus know he was dealing with a gay couple?

Of course he did. If you believe Jesus was the Son of God it is difficult to believe also that he was naïve or stupid. John (2001) points out that *the probability that the relationship was homosexual would not have escaped Jesus, Matthew or Luke.* p.159.

The patriarchal churches contort themselves trying to get out of this one, but it looks very much as if Jesus here encountered a loving homosexual relationship and gave it his blessing. More than that, he declared that this gay man had more faith than any pious observant Jew he had met, and was a model to be followed by all who truly accepted his teaching. In Matthew's account, Jesus takes the opportunity to spell out the lesson very clearly: *And I say unto you, that many shall come from the East and the West, and shall sit down with Abraham, and Isaac, and Jacob, in the Kingdom of Heaven. But the children of the kingdom shall be cast into outer darkness: there shall be weeping and gnashing of teeth.* Matthew 9:11-12.

The 'many who shall come from the East and the West' are the Gentiles, like the centurion, who are good people and obey Jesus' loving commandments. They will enter heaven 'and sit down with Abraham, Isaac and Jacob'. Those pious Jews who believed themselves as of right to be 'children of the Kingdom', simply by virtue of being Jewish and descended from Abraham, will be disappointed. It is no longer about being Jewish. It does not matter what nationality you are. And the implication of the centurion's story is that it does not matter what sexuality you are either. It was not important to Jesus that the centurion was in a relationship with another male. What was important was that the centurion had faith and acted on it. Jesus shows in both accounts absolutely no hesitation about going to cure the sick servant. What Jesus sees is not a detestable foreign soldier but a man of huge and unshakeable faith, a man full of love for his servant, and a man deeply wounded and grieved by his servant's suffering. Jesus' tribute to the gay centurion is the greatest compliment recorded anywhere in the gospels.

Jesus shocked the chief priests and elders when he told them: *Verily I say unto you that the tax collectors and the prostitutes go into the Kingdom of God before you. For John came unto you in the way of righteousness, and you believed him not; but the tax collectors and the prostitutes believe him.* Matthew 21:32.

He is promising that the disreputable and marginalised outcasts of society will get into heaven because they believed John the Baptist, whereas the self-righteous and self-satisfied Jews in the temple will not get in because they did not. As Jennings (2003) has argued, in the story of the centurion Jesus extends the Kingdom's welcome to disreputable Gentiles as well. The (Gentile) gay centurion combines in one person the distinctive characteristics of the tax collector (servant of the Gentile roman oppressor) and the prostitute (he is a pederast and sexually disreputable from a Jewish point of view). What the gay centurion does is very courageous. In his desperate love he risks rejection and ridicule to try to get help for his boyfriend from a most unlikely source. When Jesus commends him for his 'faith' he does not mean a set of codified catechistic ideas the centurion has learnt and memorised but rather: *The loving concern that draws one to take risks, to become vulnerable in hope, to reach out in yearning for well-being, to refuse to give disease or madness or paralysis the last word, to suppose that divine power is not on the side of calamity but on the side of wholeness: Jesus calls this outlook faith.* Jennings (2003) p.143.

This is why the gay centurion will go to heaven and why those who obsess about mere legalistic compliance, ritual cleanness, doctrinal orthodoxy and moral rectitude will not.

Did Jesus have a sense of humour?
There is a wry twist in the eventual ending of this story. In the daily mass celebrated in Catholic, Anglican and Orthodox churches all round the world the high point comes after the bread and wine have been consecrated as the body and blood of Christ, and the congregation are required to say aloud: *Lord I am not worthy to receive you but only say the word and I shall be healed.*

In other words, every day for the past two thousand years and continuing right up to the present, the words of faith spoken by this gay man are recalled and repeated at the most solemn and holy moment in the Church's ritual. Is this not wonderfully ironic set against the appalling treatment meted out to gay people over the centuries by these patriarchal churches?

What is the significance of this story?
This story is hugely significant even if you are not religious. The whole point of Christ's mission was to extend the salvation originally offered only to the Jews to all of humanity. Unfortunately the Christian church has resisted this universality and has sought always to exclude minorities of which it disapproved. We know that Jesus never condemned gay people. In this story we see that he blessed a man he knew to be in a gay relationship and went to extraordinary lengths to heal the man's sick lover. And ever since the church has unwittingly presided over a situation in which every time a Christian, even a homophobic Christian, receives Holy Communion he not only gets the body and blood of Christ but also the words of a gay man put into his mouth!

LGBT Self affirmation
Summary Sheet A3: Jesus meets
a Gay Couple

1. In an extraordinary encounter Jesus is asked by a powerful Roman centurion to heal his dangerously sick boy servant.
2. Linguistic analysis of the Greek words used to describe the boy servant and his relationship to the centurion strongly suggest they were what would now be termed gay lovers.
3. Jesus is utterly unconcerned with the centurion's being a hated gentile foreigner or his being in a gay relationship and immediately cures the boy.
4. Jesus is amazed by the gay centurion's faith and pays him the greatest compliment to be found in the Bible.
5. Jesus uses this story to teach the importance of faith and love and the insignificance of social identifications based on ethnic origin or kinship lineage.
6. The words of faith uttered by the gay centurion (*Lord, I am not worthy to receive you but only say the word and I shall be healed*) are recalled at the highpoint of mass and communion services when the bread and wine are consecrated as the body and blood of Christ. For homophobic Christians this is highly ironic.

The Affirmative Testament Chapter A4

The Hebrew God as a Man's Man

Yahweh seeks out handsome men

The idea that there may be anything not totally 'straight' about the Hebrew God of the Old Testament may seem prima facie absurd, given the tradition of antipathy towards homosexuality which comes down to us from Judaism through Christianity. The way that the story of Sodom and Gomorrah has been portrayed by the patriarchal churches, (wrongly, as demonstrated in chapter D1) has of course mightily reinforced the general view that Yahweh, God of Israel, is a one hundred percent 24-carat homophobe.

Recent scholarship, and most especially the seminal and groundbreaking work of Jennings (2005) on which this chapter is based, together with close scrutiny of the Biblical text however suggest that things might be a little more complex than this traditional picture suggests.

There are three key characteristics of the Hebrew God which mark him out from the gods of other cultures, for example from the gods of Ancient Greece:

He is alone;
He interacts directly with human beings;
He is particularly interested in men.

The Greek gods seem to spend a lot of their time with each other, plotting, conspiring and having adventures together in their own realm while humans are just left to get on with it down below. The single Yahweh, on the other hand, is always down at the human level on the look out for men with whom to form relationships.

We need to remember that Ancient Israel was essentially a warrior society and that its culture was preoccupied with tales of battle and derring-do in which all the characters are male. Women scarcely figure at all. And here is the key point: men, and particularly those in the most powerful roles, always appear with younger boy companions. These are often cast in the role of 'armour bearer' but their real function was to be the constant companion of their dominant partner.

Furthermore the Biblical texts make clear to us that these boy companions, these armour bearers, were not chosen for their skill in 'armour bearing' but rather for their beauty.

In this cultural context Yahweh essentially appears as a warrior chief, also in search of a companion. So for example when Saul, who Yahweh will eventually make king of Israel, first comes to his attention we are told how handsome he is: *There was a man of Benjamin......He had a son whose name was Saul, a handsome young man. There was not a man among the people of Israel more handsome than he; he stood head and shoulders above everyone else* 1 Samuel 9: 2.

We also learn that this tall handsome young man has his own youthful companion, and in the story of how he comes to meet the prophet Samuel through whom Yahweh will make Saul king we are told several times about this boy.

Once he is crowned king, Saul moves on to other armour bearers, notably David (of Goliath fame). Saul's son, Jonathan also has armour bearers, again including David. (The rivalry of father and son for the affections of David will be discussed in the next chapter).

In the course of time Saul comes to disappoint Yahweh who resolves to replace him as king. The story of how he does this is quite extraordinary from a gay perspective. He tells his prophet, Samuel, to look at each of Jesse's seven sons in turn. Having seen the first six, Samuel calls in the seventh, which of course is David, and then we read: *Now he was ruddy, and had beautiful eyes, and was handsome. The Lord said (to Samuel) "rise and anoint him; for this is the one".* 1 Samuel 16:12.

Whatever other of David's qualities might be being considered by Yahweh, the Hebrew God is clearly taken with stunning beauty of the boy (he is still a teenager at this point). Look at the detail of his eyes and his complexion. You do not need to adopt a specifically queer reading of the text to see the homoerotic implications in this kind of material.

As further confirmation of this Old Testament concern with male beauty consider also what the (male) authors of the books of 2 Samuel and 1 Kings have to say later about David's two sons: *Now in all Israel there was no one to be praised so much for his beauty as Absalom; from the sole of his foot to the crown of his head there was no blemish in him.* 2 Samuel 14:25.

He (Adonijah) was also a very handsome man, and he was born next after Absalom. 1 Kings 1:6.

The beautiful Absalom is chosen by Yahweh to carry out a curse he puts on David's house after a fall from grace, and Adonijah is assumed by Israel to have been chosen by Yahweh later to replace the then ageing, and presumably therefore no longer beautiful, David. Beauty definitely seems to be the main criterion.

Warrior-boy relationships

The treatment of Saul and of David by Yaweh carries a further implication: while the armour bearer boy companion is expected to remain totally devoted to the warrior the reverse is not true. There does here seem to be something of a parallel with heterosexual marriage at the time: a husband could have more than one wife, or serial wives, but the wife was allowed only one husband. Indeed this very parallel in pairing behaviour is itself suggestive of the homoerotic character (rather than merely homosocial) of these male-male relationships. The furious jealousy of Saul when he is displaced by his own son in the relationship with David is difficult to explain in any other terms, as will be discussed in the next chapter.

The kind of gay culture being examined here is a very macho one. These are 'men's men'. There is nothing sissy or effeminate about them. They clearly also have relations with women and sire progeny. Yahweh is in many ways an idealisation of this kind of masculine persona.

Yahweh's most significant male-male relationship is with David who eventually becomes a renowned king of Israel (and to whom the lineage of Jesus is traced back). David's life with Yahweh includes some odd scenes. There is for example the strange business of his dancing semi-naked in front of the Ark of the Covenant where Yahweh is presumed to reside.

David danced before the Lord with all his might; David was girded with a linen ephod. 2 Samuel 6:14.

An ephod is a sort of posing pouch or jock strap, leaving the buttocks exposed and possibly the genitalia still visible, at least in outline. Certainly an ephod draws attention to the genitals. As some commentators have noted (Jennings 2005) what is noteworthy is that the book of Samuel includes this story in unabridged version but the book of Chronicles which was written much later and which retells the life of David, does not. For example it has him fully clothed and accompanied. This suggests that there may well have been something erotic going on here which became shameful in a later period and which was edited out, or sanitised by the later account.

Furthermore the reaction of David's wife, who observes him prancing around, is also instructive. The text tells us that *'she despised him in her heart'* (2 Samuel 6:16). She rebukes him for *'shamelessly uncovering himself'*. One possible interpretation of her anger is that she has already had to live with her husband's involvement with Saul and with Jonathan. Now that they are dead, and she might reasonably expect his full attention, she finds him making up to another powerful male way out of her league, Yahweh himself (Jennings op cit). Perhaps she suspects that David was trying to reawaken Yahweh's desire for the beauty of his nude body. This was no ritual liturgical dance. David, however, is quite unrepentant. He feels a strong attachment to the all powerful Yahweh who has chosen him, and he implies that what he has done so far is mere foreplay: *I will make myself yet more contemptible than this, and I will be abased in my own eyes.* 2 Samuel 6:22.

What can he possibly mean, one wonders? What more can he do? The mind boggles! This does seem to be getting near to the kind of top/bottom, sub/dom behavioural styles to be found in certain parts of modern gay culture. Whatever David's actual intentions, Yahweh's response to the naked dancing is extremely positive. He basically promises David the world: security, peace, prosperity, and also posterity through the continuance of his line: *I will set up thy seed after thee, which shall proceed out of thy bowels, and I will establish his kingdom.* 2 Samuel 7:12.

Saul dances naked too

As we will discover in the next chapter, Saul eventually tries to kill David. At one point David hides in Naioth in Ramah, where the prophet Samuel and other prophets are in a frenzy. Saul sends a series of messengers to Ramah but each time 'the spirit of God' comes upon them and they end up joining the prophetic frenzy. Eventually Saul himself turns up and is afflicted in the same way: *He too stripped off his clothes, and he too fell into a frenzy before Samuel. He lay naked all that day and all that night.'* 2 Samuel 19:24.

One can only ask why? Why did he take off all his clothes for so long? The frenzy itself is seen as a sign that one has found favour with Yahweh. It is a sort of ecstatic divine possession. But remember that Saul had originally been chosen for his beauty. And now he is being displaced in Yahweh's favour by David who will replace him as king. Is this a last ditch attempt to seduce Yahweh, as his rival will later do? Moreover, the reference to 'all that day and all that night' is reminiscent of the rape suffered by the Levite's concubine, who was sexually abused *all through the night until the morning'* (Judges 19:25-27, discussed earlier in chapter D1).

Yahweh's posing pouch

It is worth noting at this point that the Bible also contains stories of Yahweh having an ephod. In chapter 8 of the Book of Judges Gideon designs a divine ephod out of gold and puts it on display, *'and all Israel went thither a-whoring after it'* (Judges 8:27). Yahweh seems to have been pleased with his new accoutrement: *Thus was Midian subdued before the children of Israel, so that they lifted up their heads no more. And the country was in quietness forty years in the days of Gideon.* Judges 8:28

And yet another divine ephod appears later in the same book. This time it is Micah who, using silver taken from his mother, *made thereof a graven image and a molten image:.....and made an ephod and a teraphim.* Judges 17:5

Whether it is that Yahweh does not like the silver ephod as much as the gold one nobody knows, but this ephod does not redound to Micah's advantage. The Danites steal it and take over his land.

What is important in these two tales, however, is that they focus attention on the way Yahweh's potency seems to arise, like his human male counterparts, from the genitals, especially the phallus. And whoever has possession of the divine ephod appears to draw on Yahweh's power and strength, and so prosper.

Yahweh's all-powerful masculinity

From these and other Old Testament stories then we learn of the immense might of Yahweh and the way in which this is linked with a kind of divine all-powerful masculinity. One of the most important of the Old Testament prophets, Elijah, draws on this potency in a most strange manner to bring a young boy back to life.

Elijah is staying with a widow whose son becomes ill and dies. Elijah takes the dead boy from the woman's arms and then carries him up to his bedroom and lays him on the bed. What happens next is really peculiar, not to say queer: *Then he stretched himself upon the child three times, and cried out to the Lord, 'O lord my God let this child's life come into him again.* 1 Kings 17:17-24

We are next told that the Lord heard Elijah's plea and restored the child to life. The obvious questions are:

why does Elijah insist on doing this in private, and
why does he get on top of the boy three times?

We need to ask what is the link between stretching out on somebody's body and the production of life? Obviously it looks like some kind of sexual act which might be real or simulated. Either way the message seems to be that somehow Elijah has channelled Yahweh's great life force into the boy's body by some kind of implied carnal engagement.

Now there is a parallel to Elijah's resurrection of the boy in the story of another prophet, confusingly named Elisha. Like Elijah, Elisha is reported as having performed many miracles. And then he too stays with a widow. She, however, is childless but Elisha makes her a promise that she will have a son despite her husband being elderly. This is in return for her hospitality towards him. In time a child is born but he too falls sick and dies in his mother's arms. She then goes upstairs and 'laid him on the bed of the man of God'. Elisha is now no longer in residence but sends his servant Gehazi who is instructed to lay his (Elisha's) staff on the boy. This does not work. Elisha comes in person, goes upstairs alone and after praying to Yahweh: *lay upon the child, putting his mouth upon his mouth, his eyes upon his eyes, and his hands upon his hands; and while he lay bent over him, the flesh of the child became warm. He got down, walked once to and for in the room, then got up again and bent over him; the child sneezed seven times, and the child opened his eyes.* Kings 4:32-35

Jennings (op cit) draws our attention to the overwhelming homoerotic overtones in this story. Obviously the staff in good Freudian tradition is a symbol for Elisha's penis. However, it looks as though without the rest of his body being there to call down the full force of Yahweh's energy the penis substitute is impotent. Is it because the real thing is needed? The degree of intimacy implied by the detailed description of body parts touching is striking, as is the erotically charged action of 'bending over'. There is even a strong sexual suggestion in the flesh of the child becoming warm. Warming flesh elsewhere in the Bible indicates a sexual arousal which signifies bodily vitality. Sneezing similarly has symbolic significance. The usual (straight) interpretation is that the author has the boy sneeze to show he was breathing but there really would be no point in this. It was enough that he was breathing. Also sneezing could denote illness or convulsions. What sneezing is like, however, is ejaculation. Physiologically the same mechanisms are involved. Sneezing seven times may not be a good sign but ejaculating seven times means you have extraordinary strength, vigour and vitality.

Elisha's relation to this boy is shrouded in uncertainty. He was responsible for the birth of the boy, perhaps in more ways than one. Now he has become the source of the boy's sexual awakening and has, either through his own action or by channelling Yahweh's sexuality, given him great sexual prowess.

These two stories of Elijah and Elisha have always represented something of a challenge to the straight censorial editors of biblical texts. Here are clearly two cases where the obvious queer reading is the only way of really making sense of what is happening.

Yaweh's sexual attacks: (1) Moses

The Bible contains a number of accounts of rape and sexual abuse. Against the background of homosexual sentiment described in this chapter it is not surprising that there are indications that some of this abuse has a homoerotic character, and indeed that some is perpetrated by Yahweh himself. Some commentators, for example, see what happens when the ark of the covenant (containing Yahweh) falls into Philistine hands as a case in point. Two days running the Philistine fertility god, Dagon, is found lying face down as if the victim of violent anal rape (1 Samuel 5:2-4). Eventually the Philistines try to rid themselves of this troublesome import but Yahweh takes further revenge by causing 'tumours to break out on them'. These tumours are believed by some to be haemorrhoids, the mark of anal rape (Ackroyd 1971).

One of the strangest and most bewildering attacks by Yahweh is on, of all people, Moses. This is set against the context of the Israelites being held captive in Egypt. Yahweh tells Moses to go to Egypt and lead his people to freedom but Moses is very reluctant, much to Yahweh's annoyance. Eventually though Moses gives in and agrees. With his family he sets off across the desert towards Egypt to do as he has been asked. However when they make camp for the night Yahweh appears and tries to kill Moses. But before he can succeed in this: *Zipporah (Moses' wife) took a flint and cut off her son's foreskin, and touched Moses' feet with it, and said, "truly you are a bridegroom of blood to me!" Yaweh let Moses alone. It was then she said, "a bridegroom of blood by circumcision".* Exodus 4:24-26

Why on earth would Yahweh do this just when Moses had begun to do what he wanted him to do? Bizarrely it looks like another instance of sexual jealousy.

What Zipporah is doing is telling Yahweh to back off because Moses belongs to her. She takes blood from her son's penis and applies it to her husband's penis. 'Feet' is a recognised substitute in biblical language for penis (cf Ruth 3:4 discussed in later chapter A7, Isaiah 6:2, Isaiah 7:20). As her bridegroom of circumcised blood she has exclusive rights to him and Yahweh therefore no longer has any. The blood may also signify the consummation of the marriage reproducing the blood of the first intercourse when Zipporah was a virgin. An alternative view is that the blood now on Moses' penis represents menstrual blood thus rendering him ritually unclean and unavailable for sexual purposes. Under the Leviticus code of holiness it was forbidden for men to have sex with menstruating women. The idea here would be that Yahweh would now recoil from any contact with Moses.

Even though the text tells us that Yahweh wanted to kill Moses this again looks more like a violent sexual attack which Zipporah frustrates, rather than a case of attempted murder. Moses of course goes on to have a deep and intimate relationship with Yahweh. He is reported to have seen Yahweh face to face and even mouth to mouth. Most strangely on one occasion he is also given sight of the divine posterior: *I will put thee in a clift of the rock, and will cover thee with my hand while I pass by; and I will take away mine hand, and thou shalt see my back parts: but my face shall not be seen.* Exodus 33:22-23

What a very bizarre vision this conjures up! Yahweh provocatively uncovers his bottom so that Moses can get a glimpse of it through the hole in a rock wall without seeing his face! Gay men all over the world will be able to identify with such anonymous titillation. But for the macho Warrior Chieftain of all macho Warrior Chieftains, reputedly and reportedly most homophobic of all homophobes, this truly is very queer behaviour indeed. God in a gloryhole!

Yaweh's sexual attacks: (2) Jacob's wound

Jacob is the father of Joseph (of dreamcoat fame) whose story is told in chapter A5. Jacob has tricked his brother Esau out of his rightful inheritance and gone off in search of a wife. He returns with wives in the plural, mistresses, children and cattle but is fearful of Esau's reaction. So he decides to wait at the boundary of the land and send gifts ahead to Esau to appease him. While he is in this no-man's land, neither inside the boundary of the territory nor properly outside it, he has a strange encounter.

And Jacob was left alone; and there wrestled a man with him until the breaking of the day. And when he saw that he prevailed not against him, he touched the hollow of his thigh; and the hollow of Jacob's thigh was out of joint, as he wrestled with him. And he said, let me go, for the day breaketh. And he said, I will not let thee go except thou bless me.
Genesis 32:24-26

This is a remarkable and savage battle. Jacob struggles against the unknown stranger all night. Somehow this is also linked to Jacob's success in deceiving his father, Isaac and his brother, Esau. This has emboldened Jacob and made him strong, so strong that the assailant cannot 'prevail' against him. But what the assailant does do is to wound Jacob in the thigh area. This actually leaves him with a permanent limp, by which he is forever recognizable thereafter. At the end of the story we are told that to this day the Israelites do not eat the thigh muscle in recognition of the wound inflicted on Jacob. Rabbinic commentators think that what was damaged was actually Jacob's sciatic nerve, which runs down the back of the top of the leg from under the buttocks near the rectal cavity of the hip bones. This injury is consistent with the damage which can be inflicted by a violent homosexual attack.

Of course it looks like Yahweh up to his old tricks again! This is clearly no ordinary human assailant. Like vampires and other ghosts and ghoulies he needs to leave before daybreak. But somehow he has transmitted to Jacob a superhuman strength from which he himself cannot escape. This sounds very similar to the transference of life force through some kind of sexual assault discussed earlier. The deal then is that Jacob will let him go provided Yahweh gives him a blessing. Yahweh asks him what his name is. Jacob explains that he is so called because the name means 'the supplanter'. Yahweh gives him a blessing and a new name, Israel, which means 'one who strives with God'. This is an extraordinary outcome. Jacob/Israel is injured and will always limp but he is now to be the father of the nation. Yahweh will ensure that the offspring of Jacob's sons are fruitful from generation to generation.

And so we are forced to consider the possibility that there in the Bible stands a seminal story which suggests the Jewish nation was founded in a night long homosexual struggle with the Hebrew God. If there is any kind of truth in this reading of the story it represents a cruel irony of history of colossal proportions. Just think for a moment of all the thousands of Jewish lesbian women and Jewish gay men who have been taught to hate themselves, who have been excluded, persecuted and murdered in the last four thousand years in the name of a God who spent the night 'wrestling' with the first Israelite.

LGBT Self affirmation
Summary Sheet A4: The Hebrew God
as a Man's Man

1. The Hebrew God is unusual – alone, interacts directly with humans, focuses on men

2. The men he chooses are selected on the criterion of male beauty.

3. In Ancient Israel it was normal for warriors to have boy companions chosen for their appearance.

4. David has a particularly erotic relationship with Yahweh, dancing semi naked in front of him.

5. Some Israelites paid particular attention to Yahweh's genitalia and made images of a divine posing pouch (ephod)

6. Elijah and Elisha bring boys back to life and vitality by calling on Yahweh whilst in some kind of sexual congress with them.

7. Yaweh launches an apparently sexual attack on Moses but is foiled by his wife applying blood from her son's foreskin to Moses' penis.

8. Jacob's wound from the night of struggle ('wrestling') with Yahweh is consistent with a violent homosexual attack. He is renamed Israel and becomes the founder of a nation as his reward.

The Affirmative Testament Chapter A5

David, Jonathan and Saul

Many people have heard of the story of the love between David and Jonathan. What is less well-known is the love story concerning David and Saul which preceded it.

Saul is Jonathan's father. He is the King of Israel, anointed as such by Yahweh, the Hebrew God of the Old Testament, who delighted in Saul's strength and beauty as a young man. Unfortunately King Saul incurs God's displeasure when he fails to exterminate every last Amalekite during a crucial battle. As we have seen in the previous chapter, God is something of a barbarous warrior-chieftain at this stage in the history of Israel. He resolves to replace Saul with David, a young man again chosen for his exceptional beauty. (1 Samuel 16:12)

In the Book of Samuel we are given two accounts of how God arranges for David to come to Saul's attention. This is not unusual in the Old Testament where through generations of retelling stories get transformed and jumbled together.

First version: David is chosen to become Saul's armour bearer

Saul is said to have been possessed by an evil spirit and is given to fits of mad rage which frighten the royal household. His servants tell him about David who is an accomplished player of the harp and whose lovely music can soothe the king. This works well and 1 Samuel 16:21-23 tell us: *And David came to Saul, and stood before him, and he loved him greatly, and he became his armour bearer.* 1 Samuel 16:12.

The role of armour bearer at that time meant a lasting close emotional homoerotic bond that was established between an older warrior and a handsome younger male, chosen for his good looks, who would be his constant companion. Saul says to David's father, Jesse: *Let David remain in my service, for he has found favour in my sight.*

As Helminiak (2000) points out, contrary to popular belief David was not really an ordinary shepherd boy. He was the son of a politically astute father well used to the machinations of power and influence in Jewish society. It could well be that David, far from being the naïve yokel some think, actually set out to seduce Saul as a way of gaining entry to the court. Later when he himself becomes king he shows political shrewdness quite at variance with the image of an innocent shepherd boy. One possible interpretation of these verses is that when David appears before Saul he does so blatantly with an erection ('standing before him') so heightening Saul's interest in him, and leading to the declaration that David has 'found favour in my sight'. And 'finding favour' is another indicator of a strong emotional attachment with a suggestion of intimacy.

In recent scholarly research into these texts there are some tantalising suggestions about their meaning. A major problem in interpreting the two books of Samuel is that they have been repeatedly edited and reedited. Consequently there is no coherent narrative, and the text we have now is full of distortions, repetitions, and inconsistencies. A further problem is the absence of vowels in Hebrew, meaning that the written words can be interpreted in numerous different ways, e.g. in English fnd could mean fend, find, fund, fond or fined.

Helminiak quotes work by the scholar Kamal Salibi which explores these possible meanings. He shows that only one assumed vowel supports the standard version of 1 Samuel 16:21 'David came to Saul and stood before him'. Of course the idea is already ambiguous, but with a different assumed vowel the verb becomes reflexive and the *actual* meaning in the Hebrew is then 'had an erection before Saul.' Similarly in the standard version of

1 Samuel 18:12, 'Saul was afraid of David, because the Lord was with him' could mean 'because he had been in love with him'. And when the prophet Samuel later criticises Saul he says to him, assuming different vowels in 1 Samuel 15:23, 'surely thrusts in the rear are an offense'. Salibi also argues that Saul's later giving of his daughter Michal to David was just a cover for the relationship between the two.

Second version: David and Goliath

During a war with the Philistines David, who is only a boy at the time, brings food for his older brothers who are serving in Saul's army. David is, however, brave and has fought lions and bears in his role as shepherd. The Philistine's champion is the giant Goliath, of whom everyone is afraid. David steps forward and: *when the Philistine looked and saw David he disdained him for he was only a youth, ruddy and handsome in appearance.* 1 Samuel 17:42, but, nevertheless, David famously fells the giant with one stone from his sling. Saul is very taken with him and invites him to be his armour bearer.

David meets Jonathan

Although we are told Saul loved David he quickly comes to feel murderous towards him. This may be because David's great successes as a warrior make him very popular with the people and Saul's jealousy of him grows. *All Israel and Judah loved David; for it was he who marched out and came in leading them.* 1 Samuel 18:16.

Equally probable, however, is that almost as soon as the ageing King Saul employs David as his boy-companion a rival for David's affections emerges in the shape of Jonathan, Saul's own eldest son.

When David and Jonathan first meet it looks very like love at first sight. *When David had finished speaking to Saul, the soul of Jonathan was bound to the soul of David, and Jonathan loved him as his own soul.* 1 Samuel 18:1-2.

What possible explanation can there be for this instant 'binding of souls' other than immediate sexual attraction? It is not the words David spoke to Jonathan as these were of mind-numbing banality, simply describing who he is and who his father is. The reader has already been made aware of David's great beauty and this is apparently the explanation. Jonathan is at pains to express his delight in David and gives him his most treasured possessions: *Jonathan stripped himself of the robe that he was wearing, and gave it to David, and his armour and even his sword and his bow and his belt.* 1 Samuel 18:4.

This looks for all the world like a touching and humble submission before a beloved.

These are all the symbols of power which Jonathan holds by virtue of his position as heir to the throne, and he gives them to David. This is an act which it is difficult to understand in any other terms than a profound expression of great love.

Saul's jealous anger

And in this way an extraordinary rivalry is established between King Saul and his heir apparent for the affections of the beautiful young shepherd boy. Saul's jealous rages are now also directed towards his own son. *Then Saul's anger was kindled against Jonathan. He said to him, 'you son of a perverse rebellious woman! Do I not know that you have chosen the son of Jesse to your own shame, and to the shame of your mother's nakedness?!'* 1 Samuel 20:30

In the biblical context, especially in the holiness code of Leviticus, the revelation of someone's shame and their nakedness denotes the consequences of sexual acts. In his anger, this is what Saul is referring to: *You shall not uncover the nakedness of your father, which is the nakedness of your mother; she is your mother, you shall not uncover her nakedness. You shall not uncover the nakedness of your father's wife; it is the nakedness of your father.* Leviticus 18:7-8.

It is probable that the implication here is by having an erotic or even sexual relationship with David, Jonathan is uncovering 'his father's nakedness' because Saul has already also had sexual relations with David. And by so uncovering his father's nakedness Jonathan also uncovers the nakedness of another with whom Saul has had sexual relations: his wife, Jonathan's own mother. Saul's outburst does not seem to make any sense unless he has also 'known' David 'in the biblical sense'. So at the same time as he is effectively calling his son a queer he is also revealing that he too has had a homosexual liaison with David.

Jonathan and David swear a covenant

In this situation the ageing King Saul's anger and resentment against David is intensified. He has effectively been jilted by David, and this has also destroyed his relationship with his son. Because of their great bravery and courage in battle both David and Jonathan are loved by the fighting troops whereas the weakened and indecisive Saul is no longer fully trusted or respected. Saul pursues David in an attempt to kill him. But twice during these battles David gains the upper hand and finds himself in a position to kill Saul. Yet David spares him on both occasions, thereby suggesting that he still feels some affection for Saul and demonstrating the loyalty and steadfastness for which he becomes famed. The main effect of Saul's hostility is to push David more and more into the arms of Jonathan: *'Thus Jonathan made a covenant with the house of David saying, "may the Lord seek out the enemies of David". Jonathan made David swear again by his love for him; for he loved him as he loved his own life.'* (1 Samuel 20: 13-17).

Later we are told that *'they kissed each other, and wept with each other; David wept the more. 1 Samuel 20:41-42.*

This really is romance of a high order. The strong implication is that they are crying because they are about to be separated from each other. Because of the danger to his life David is obliged to take refuge with Saul's enemies, the Philistines. He does not, however, fight with them against Saul's Israelite armies, once again demonstrating his enduring faithfulness to the father and son who loved him, even in the face of extreme provocation. This means that he is not there when both Saul and Jonathan are killed on the battlefield. When he hears of this David is utterly grief stricken and cries out: *I am distressed for you, my brother Jonathan; greatly beloved were you to me; your love to me was wonderful, passing the love of women.* 2 Samuel 1: 25-26.

This reference here to 'the love of women' clearly identifies this relationship as having an erotic character. In those days men did not 'do friendship' with women. After Jonathan's death David later shows further his deep love for Jonathan in adopting and protecting Jonathan's son for the rest of his life. Once more then we encounter a gay love story in the 'good book', one which is rarely spoken of by the patriarchal churches, and yet one which proves conclusively that the Bible is far from being the homophobic text unremittingly hostile to homosexual relationships which is how these churches tend to represent it.

Were both David and Jonathan gay?

It has been suggested that, while Jonathan seems unequivocally homosexual in orientation, David may have been more sexually ambiguous. The Book of Samuel paints a picture of Jonathan being 'head over heels' in love with David, literally willing to give his lover the world. And there is no indication of Jonathan ever expressing any interest at all in women. David, on the other hand, ends up married to a woman. However, the background to this marriage needs to be clearly understood.

Saul first offers David the hand of his eldest daughter, Meroh, but David declines. Saul next offers his younger daughter, Michal, and again David says no. Saul doubtless had his own reasons for wanting to keep David in the family. Later, however, David reconsiders and changes his mind. Conceivably it dawned on him how politically useful to his future advancement it would be to have the king for a father-in-law. But there is nothing approaching lust for females in any of this. There is no reference to the beauty or attractiveness of these women. This is all hard-headed expediency calculation. Samuel's text tells us that 'Michal loved David' but we are never told that David loved Michal, probably because he didn't. We have already seen something of their less than happy domestic bliss in the previous chapter.

Thus far from being 'gay for pay' (or at least material advantage) in his relationship with Jonathan, it is more a case of David being straight for gain in his marriage to Michal. The Biblical evidence is that David and Jonathan were the real thing. Michal was the convenient contrivance.

This was actually love between two men in the fullest sense, grounded in homoerotic desire but overlain with deep emotion and enduring commitment. It is a covenant which is kept and fulfilled by both men until the end of their days. Tom Horner (1978) in his celebrated book 'Jonathan Loved David' likened their relationship to that between Gilgamesh, King of Uruk, and Enkidu, his inseparable companion, whose love was well known throughout the Middle East in ancient times. Describing Gilgamesh's inconsolable distress when his lover dies, Horner comments: *No mourner in the history of the world – except perhaps Alexander at the passing of his friend Hephaestion – has ever been more broken up over the loss of his (or her) beloved friend .*

David's words of utter devastation when Jonathan is killed follow precisely in this tradition of male love. And, significantly, at no point in the narrative is there any word of criticism from the Hebrew God. On the contrary, the Lord lavishes favours upon David, leading him to the throne where he will become the greatest king of Ancient Israel. And from the line of David will eventually be born in Bethlehem the Saviour of the world. If ever a man was blessed by God it was David, and this despite his involvement in at least two homosexual affairs. This is truly an inspirational story for all gay people everywhere.

LGBT Self affirmation
Summary Sheet A5: David, Jonathan and Saul

1. The first version of how David comes to the notice of King Saul is through musicianship, playing the harp to soothe his rages.
2. Some scholars believe David stood before Saul with an erection.
3. The second version of how David comes to the notice of King Saul is by killing Goliath with his sling.
4. When David meets Jonathan, King Saul's son, it is love at first sight.
5. Jonathan gifts to David all the symbols of his royal status: robe, armour, sword, bow and belt.
6. Saul becomes jealous and in so doing reveals his own sexual attachment to David.
7. David and Jonathan kiss and weep and enter a solemn covenant with each other. Jonathan loved David *'as he loved his own life'*.
8. David is devastated when Jonathan is killed and says he loved him with a wonderful love *'passing the love of women'*.
9. The relationship between David and Jonathan is accepted as normal by the surrounding society.
10. There is no criticism from the Lord of any of these relationships. Indeed David is favoured by God and anointed eventually as king, going on to become the greatest king in the Old Testament.

The Affirmative Testament Chapter A6

Joseph the Transvestite

In his review of homoerotic narrative in the literature of Ancient Israel Theodore Jennings (2005) identifies the story of Joseph and his brothers as one in which there are hidden LGBT implications to be drawn out. He suggests that there are several elements which imply that this is not the straightforward happy, feel good saga of happy family life depicted in the standard version and the celebrated musical.

Joseph's coat was a dress

The one thing everybody thinks they know about Joseph is that he had a coat of many colours, or a 'technicolor dreamcoat' as the musical written by Tim Rice and Andrew Lloyd Webber has it. Like so many things that 'everybody knows' about the Bible it is not quite right.

The most important thing about Joseph's coat is not so much that it was multicoloured but that it was a 'long robe with long sleeves' as more recent theological scholarship and research has revealed. Three times in the Genesis text which recounts Joseph's story we are told that the robe is 'long' and 'with sleeves'.

What is the point of this repetition? What it does is draw attention to the fact that the robe is actually female clothing. Exactly the same descriptions are used for dresses worn by the king's daughters in 2 Samuel 13: 18-19, including Tamar the princess: *'Now she was wearing a long robe with sleeves of divers colours; for this is how the virgin daughters of the King were clothed in earlier times.'*

Thus Joseph's coat is not just feminine it is also the distinguishing mark of a royal female virgin. And what makes this story even queerer is that this princess' robe is specifically given to Joseph by his father, the patriarch Jacob, who regarded him as possessing great beauty and loved him more than any other of his brothers.

Now Jacob loved Joseph more than any other of his children, because he was the son of his old age; and he had made him a long robe with sleeves. But when his brothers saw that their father loved him more than all his brothers, they hated him, and could not speak peaceably to him. Genesis 37:3-4

It does seem a strange thing for a patriarchal father to do. As we have seen in earlier chapters gender boundaries were very strong in Ancient Israel, and cross dressing was specifically forbidden in the Jewish Holiness code on pain of death. Jacob surely cannot have been unaware of the implications of dressing his youngest son up in this way. And yet perhaps he was following in a cultural tradition. As Jennings observes, this act of Jacob's is in keeping with some of the characteristic Old Testament homoerotic affection discussed earlier: *The remarkably lovely adolescent male is transgendered by the affection of a more powerful male.* (p.181)

Gaybashing

Whatever Jacob's motivations, this dress casts the story of Joseph in an entirely different light. When he first appears in the Biblical text he is seventeen, just entering manhood, a process stopped in its tracks by his father's dressing him in female apparel. The garment marks Joseph out as not in the role of a 'real man', not out on the land with the sheep like his brothers, but rather having a domestic and even ornamental function like a girl or woman of that time.

It may well therefore be this, rather than the paternal favouritism or his annoying habit of telling them about his grandiose dreams in which they bow down to him, which is the real reason his brothers hate Joseph so much. It is not accidental that the first thing they do to him when they attack him is to rip the girl's dress off him. They then tear up this offensive symbol of cross dressing and spoiled masculinity and throw their gender bending brother into a pit. This callous aggression is arguably the first instance of overt gaybashing in the Bible.

When the brothers give the torn dress, now covered in blood, to Jacob his reaction is quite astonishing. He tears his own clothes to pieces and bizarrely then puts sackcloth on his own private parts, as if to show that his grief for the lovely boy is particularly poignant for him in his sexual organs. In every sense of the word, this seems a decidedly queer thing to do and raises serious questions about the nature of Jacob's relationship with his pretty boy son.

Protection by powerful men

The brothers sell Joseph into slavery and he is taken to Egypt where he 'finds favour' under a series of powerful males. We have seen already in the story of David, Jonathan and Saul that the expression 'find favour' is a metaphor for sexual attraction.

First is Potiphar, 'the captain of the guard', to whom he becomes a sort of personal assistant. Again the reader is reminded that Joseph is 'handsome and good looking'. The Biblical text suggests that Joseph was popular with both Potiphar and his wife, and his career advances rapidly as he becomes overseer of the whole household. When, however, Potiphar's wife 'casts her eyes' on him and asks Joseph 'to lie with her', he wants none of it. This may be out of discretion or it may be because he feels no sexual desire for her as a woman. And when she traps him in her bedroom and all but assaults him, he runs off in desperation leaving her hanging on to the garment he was wearing.

Because she then makes false accusations against him he finds himself in prison, where he is befriended by the chief jailer with whom once again this beautiful lad 'finds favour'. Of course such protection in prisons is not unknown even today. And later he comes to the attention of the Pharoah, who in gratitude for Joseph's interpretation of his dreams, makes him his prime male favourite, and *'removing his signet ring from his hand, Pharoah put it on Joseph's hand; he arrayed him in garments of fine linen, and put a gold chain around his neck.* Genesis 41:42

It is as if Joseph now becomes the favoured consort, almost like a kind of wife, to the Egyptian ruler. In each of these cases of 'protection and favour' we have to ask why? What is the pay off for each powerful man? That it happens four times in quick succession, Jacob, Potiphar, the Jailer, Pharoah, points strongly to an obvious conclusion. Joseph was the object of their erotic desire.

Joseph as female or eunuch?

Throughout his life Joseph appears notably disinterested in sex with women, in stark contrast to his lusty brothers, especially Reuben, the eldest, who even sleeps with his father's concubine. Joseph, on the other hand, never seeks out the company of women and flees when Potpihar's wife begins her amorous advances towards him. His focus seems to be exclusively on using his unusual beauty to 'find favour' with significant males, Jacob, Potiphar, the Chief Jailer and the Pharoah, to each of whom he is in some sense a toyboy. There is even the suggestion in the text that he does this quite consciously and deliberately. Before he appears for the first time in front of Pharoah, for example, he goes to some lengths to make an impact: *When he had shaved himself and changed his clothes, he came in before Pharoah.* Genesis 41:14

This may seem a commonplace but we have to ask ourselves why the author would bother to tell us this apparently trivial detail if it did not indicate something about Joseph. Such mundane actions would not normally be mentioned. The point is that Joseph is (suspiciously) fussy about his appearance, he wants to look good, he wants to catch the Pharoah's eye. And clearly he succeeds. His preoccupation with his looks and image is somewhat unmanly and revealing. He acts as though he were a female or a eunuch.

Eventually though the Pharoah gives him a wife, as was the custom, and it seems as if he is being transformed by the Genesis author finally into a heterosexual character. Two sons arrive, Ephraim and Manasseh, but then there is a quite unexpected and bizarre twist to the story which once again casts serious doubt over Joseph's sexuality.

After the brothers, as foretold in Joseph's childhood dreams, come shamefacedly to beg for Egyptian food from the now powerful Joseph, contact is thereby renewed with the ageing father, Jacob. There then ensues a most odd scene in which Jacob says *'your two sons who were born to you in the land of Egypt...are now mine; Ephraim and Manassah shall be mine, just as Reuben and Simeon are'. (Genesis 48:5)*

He sits the boys on his lap and then Joseph receives them back from him, as though he were the wife/mother. Some commentators have described this act as the 'erasure' of Joseph's paternity. The sons of Joseph are transmuted into the sons of Jacob. Jennings (op.cit.) contends that it is as if Joseph has been a cross-dressing eunuch all along, and has in the end become a surrogate wife to his father Jacob, in place of his now dead mother, Rachel.

A queer hero

Joseph's life is lived out in peculiar ambivalences and ambiguities: a male in female clothing, a father deprived of his offspring, a slave exercising authority on behalf of powerful men, ambiguously positioned in relation to his family and defined gender roles. He is a truly queer figure, and one displaying many admirable qualities. He shows courage, resourcefulness, determination, loyalty, steadfastness and magnanimity. Despite their appalling behaviour towards him he forgives his brothers and is gracious towards them. Against all the odds he is hugely successful. He is in many ways a great Biblical queer hero whose trials and tribulations and whose successes and joys everyone can affirm and celebrate.

But for LGBT people in particular, Joseph is, in the words of that great song from *La Cage aux Folles*, 'his own special creation'. To do justice to Joseph's story a new musical is needed, less saccharin and self satisfied, more gritty and hard-edged, to portray this remarkable character in his full glory. He is an outsider who does not belong, but he takes control of his own destiny and shows the world proudly who he is and what he can do, even in the face of all that it throws at him. He navigates his way dextrously through the minefield that is patriarchal culture if you are a sexual dissident. In the next chapter we shall meet two gay women who appear to manage the same trick.

LGBT Self affirmation
Summary Sheet A6: Joseph the Transvestite

1. Joseph's coat of many colours was actually an item of female clothing typically worn by virgin princesses in Old Testament times.

2. This dress was given to him by his father, Jacob, because he loved Joseph best of all his many sons. It marked Joseph out as different and put him more in a female domestic role than the 'normal' masculine role as he entered adulthood.

3. The brutal resentment of Joseph's brothers may have been as much due to his being 'girly' as to his dreams or his father's favouritism. Their attack on him would then amount to gaybashing.

4. Three times Joseph is 'befriended' by powerful males, a pattern of behaviour raising clear doubts about his sexuality:
    a) Potiphar, the captain of the guard
    b) the chief jailer
    c) the Egyptian Pharoah

5. Joseph runs away when Potiphar's wife offers him sex.

6. Somehow his own eventual two sons end up not being his, but becoming his father's, which is very queer indeed.

The Affirmative Testament Chapter A7

Ruth and Naomi

Naomi meets Ruth

During a terrible famine in the land of Judah, Naomi and her husband and their two sons move to Moab in search of food. They put down roots as immigrants and eventually the two sons marry local Moabite women. Sadly, however, Naomi's husband and both sons die. With the passage of time, the famine in Judah is over and Naomi now decides to return alone to her native land, hoping that she will be able to find some of her family still alive there to look after her in her later years.

Her two Moabite daughters-in-law though have come to love her and demand to go with her, to become immigrant aliens in her land just as she has been in Moab. Naomi tries to dissuade them by pointing out that moving to Judah would make it difficult for them to find new husbands. *The Lord grant you that ye may find rest, each of you in the house of her husband. Then she kissed them; and they lifted up their voice, and wept. And they said unto her, surely we will return with thee to thy people.* Ruth 1:9 -10

One daughter-in-law, Orpah, reluctantly agrees but the other, Ruth, 'clings to her' *And they lifted up their voice, and wept again: and Orpah kissed her mother-in-law; but Ruth clave unto her.* Ruth 1:14.

Ruth refuses to leave Naomi

Naomi tries once again to get Ruth to see sense and attempts to persuade her to stay behind but Ruth resists. She is determined not to be separated from the woman she has come to love, and she utters this famous hymn to her beloved: *Entreat me not to leave you or to return from following after you; for where you go I will go, and where you lodge I will lodge; your people shall be my people, and your God my God; where you die I will die, and there I will be buried. May the Lord do so to me and more also if even death parts me from you.* Ruth 1:16-17

This beautiful little speech has come to be a great favourite at wedding ceremonies, signifying as it does great love and loyalty. How many brides and bridegrooms, one wonders, realise that these words were actually spoken by a woman to another woman? What we apparently have here is an unashamed declaration of same-sex love being used as a statement of committed heterosexual love. It in fact goes even further than the 'till death us do part' pledge in the marriage service, asking God to continue the union after the partners have died.

The word usually translated as 'clung' is *(dabaq)* is the same word used in Genesis to describe heterosexual marriage: *Therefore a man leaves his father and mother and cleaves (dabaq) to his wife, and they become one flesh.* Genesis 2:24

Note the parallel here that Ruth, like the man, is leaving her home community to be with the object of her 'cleaving'. Later in the story Ruth's future husband, Boaz, will confirm this parallel, telling Ruth that he knows all about what she has done for Naomi in 'leaving your father and mother and your native land (2:11). Note also that Ruth has chosen to be with Naomi in preference to remaining in Moab to find another man to marry, a clear indication that her relationship with Naomi is an equivalent to heterosexual marriage.

Naomi fixes a cover marriage for Ruth

Nonetheless Ruth does find a husband in Judah but in a rather strange manner which protects rather than threatens her relationship with Naomi. Naomi organises everything and tells Ruth how to seduce the ageing but wealthy Boaz. *Wash thyself therefore, and anoint thee, and put thy raiment upon thee, and get thee down to the floor: but make not thyself known unto the man, until he*

shall have done eating and drinking. And it shall be, when he lieth down that thou shalt make the place where he shall lie, and thou shalt go in, and uncover his feet, and lay thee down; and he will tell thee what thou shalt do. And she said unto her, All that thou sayest unto me I will do.
Ruth 3: 3-5

As we have seen before, the use of the word 'feet' is often intended as a proxy for the genitalia. Clearly Ruth is being asked to stimulate Boaz sexually. The text here is very odd with an apparent confusion between 'you' and 'I' so that it reads as if Naomi/Ruth is one person. You could say that they have become *'one flesh'* as in the Genesis text above.

But the plan works very well. Boaz is very grateful for the attention lavished on him, imagining that Ruth might have offered herself to a younger man. He seems blithely unaware that this would not at all have suited the women's plans. Naomi's intention is to find in Ruth's marriage to Boaz a shelter within which the two women can safely continue their relationship in the context of a rigidly heterosexist patriarchal society.

This protective situation is unaffected by the birth of a son, Obed. Indeed there are further peculiarities in the textual description which reinforce idea that the two women are unusually close. It is as if the local women of the village have understood what is going on. They declare: *There is a son born to Naomi.* Ruth 4:17

This little sentence is itself pregnant with implications for this story of same sex love.

One possible interpretation of it is that the townswomen have made a mistake and attributed the new baby to the wrong woman. This is unlikely. They would have been sufficiently close to the 'action' to know from whose womb the baby emerged.

So what does it mean? If they are fully aware that Ruth is the biological mother, why do they say a son is born to Naomi? Some commentators have suggested that because of the relationship the townswomen perceive between the two women they view

Naomi as the father of the child. Obviously Naomi cannot literally be the father in the sense of having provided the sperm. If the townswomen treat Naomi as the 'father' this can only be in the sense of giving public recognition to her parental status because they see the baby is born into the relationship between the two women, rather than into the marriage between Ruth and Boaz. But Naomi is also somehow the mother of the child because it is she who nurses him *And Naomi took the child, and laid it in her bosom, and became nurse unto it.* Ruth 4:16

The townswomen, remarkably, seem willing to live with the astonishing degree of gender role ambiguity which characterises this ménage à trois. It is as if they realise the marriage between Ruth and Boaz is a sham, and that the real 'becoming one flesh' occurs between the two women.

The two women thrive in a patriarchal society

In this way, just as earlier in the story, Ruth behaved like a man in 'leaving father and mother to cleave' to Naomi, now Naomi also appears to be being transgendered into either a male role or some kind of transsexual androgynous role. All of this points to the ongoing intimacy of the two female lovers under the safety blanket of Ruth's marriage to Boaz and the production of a son, the two essential requirements of a fertile woman in a patriarchal culture. Having satisfied these two criteria, the two women are left free and undisturbed to enjoy and take delight in each other's company. It is telling that while the text informs us that Ruth loved Naomi, it never tells us that Ruth loved her husband, Boaz. And she clearly does not. The whole way in which, acting on Naomi's instructions, Ruth coldly, calculatingly and deliberately seduces Boaz makes it clear that she is not in the least attracted emotionally or sexually to this man. She is not doing this for him or for herself but for Naomi. Later the baby is taken away from the Ruth/Boaz relationship and assimilated into the Ruth/Naomi relationship.

There is no suggestion in the story that Boaz has any idea that he is merely a provider of social and economic security to the two female lovers. He thinks a son has been born to him even if all the townswomen know better. And oddly it is these townswomen rather than he who name the boy: *And the women her neighbours gave it a name........and they called his name Obed: he is the father of Jesse, the father of David.* Ruth 4:17

As is evident in this verse, this boy will become the progenitor of a line which will eventually lead to the birth of Jesus Christ. Here then is one more LGBT relevant fact that is seldom noticed or remarked on: one of Jesus' ancestors was born to and raised by a lesbian couple.

It is probable that the story of Ruth and Noami is a paradigm for how lesbian relationships survive in male dominated society. The men are so focussed on fulfilling the exacting demands of the male role within the structure of power that they simply do not notice the female relationships being enjoyed all around them.

In this story the two women cleverly manipulate the situation in which they find themselves to arrive at an ideal outcome for their partnership. Naomi is greatly respected by everybody and Ruth is loved and accepted into Naomi's community. Almost everybody seems to know what is really going on. Even the ageing Boaz may simply be turning a blind eye because the arrangement suits him so well. It really is extraordinary that he does not object to Naomi's 'intrusion' into his marriage with Ruth, and even more bizarre that he says nothing when the townswomen name his son. One wonders what the other men around Boaz thought but the Bible is silent on this point. Presumably if they were troubled the reader would have been told. And of course the other significant silence is the Lord's. There is no comment or condemnation from Yahweh either.

No condemnation of this same sex relationship

The absence of any hint of criticism of this domestic arrangement which, if lived out now, would outrage contemporary evangelical Christians, is of great significance. Conservative evangelicals of course believe that the Bible is the literal word of God, and presumably therefore the silence of God when he definitely should not be silent is also literal truth. In this case the literal truth appears to be that God is not bothered by the goings on between Ruth, Naomi, Boaz and the local women. You could call this God giving his blessing by default.

It is an intriguing question as to why the divine wrath is not provoked by these two women who loved each other. Evangelical Christians argue constantly, volubly and virulently that God hates homosexuals and yet here to all intents and purposes are two lesbians living together and having their relationship recognised, accepted and fully approved by God's own people. And more, they give birth and bring up a child together who will be the grandfather of the great King David, which would certainly not have happened if Yahweh's displeasure had been incurred.

Not only is there not one iota of disapproval from anybody, but these women are positively rewarded with wealth, happiness and complete integration into Jewish society. Proof, if any more were needed, that homosexuality per se is not the issue and never has been. The issue, as in all these Bible stories is patriarchy, and what distinguishes these two gay women is their understanding of how patriarchal society functions and their skill in working within its parameters rather than against them. That is why they survive, thrive and flourish. Those who come to grief are those who openly challenge patriarchal domination, something which Naomi and Ruth, like Joseph in the previous chapter, managed with great adroitness to avoid.

It is quite clear that these two women were in what would now be called a gay marriage. The vow that Ruth makes to Naomi when she refuses to be left behind in Moab captures perfectly the essence of marital love, which is of course why it is used so often at weddings. That it is so often so used indeed confirms precisely the marital love these two women felt for each other. The Reverend Nancy Wilson (1995) has argued that LGBT people should interrupt any straight weddings they attend where Ruth's vow is being used and say: *STOP, in the name of Ruth and Naomi.....! Stop stealing our stories while making our relationships illegal or characterizing them as immoral!* P157.

It is certainly ironic that the most Christian churches nowadays would stop two women making the vow which Ruth makes to Naomi in the Bible.

The churches claim that the story of Ruth and Naomi is only about friendship, not sexual love. This is a case of double standards. If the vow does not imply sexual love why do the churches preside over its use at heterosexual weddings between avowedly sexual lovers? And if the vow does not imply sexual love would they allow two women to make it if they promised to remain celibate? Of course not. This is quite a good litmus test for the naked homophobia which underpins so much church teaching.

LGBT Self affirmation
Summary Sheet A7: Ruth and Naomi

1. Naomi resolves to return home from Moab after the death of her husband and both her sons.
2. Naomi's daughter-in-law Ruth loves her and begs not to be left behind using words now famous and widely used at weddings to express spousal love.
3. Ruth cleaves to Naomi as a husband cleaves to his wife (the Bible uses the same Hebrew word).
4. Naomi instructs Ruth in how to seduce Boaz so that they can continue their relationship under the protective cover of a patriarchal marriage.
5. The local women understand what is going on and attribute the birth of a child to Naomi even though Ruth is the biological mother.
6. It is the local women who name the boy Obed, not Boaz the biological father.
7. There is no hint of criticism in the text from anybody in the story. Crucially for the patriarchal churches there is no condemnation from the Lord. Ruth and Naomi are accepted and thrive in Jewish society.
8. Obed will become grandfather to the future King David from whose line Jesus Christ is born centuries later. The Son of God thus possibly descends from a baby born to and raised by two lesbians.
9. The Rev Nancy Wilson believes LGBT people should challenge the use of Ruth's hymn of love to Naomi at heterosexual marriages.

The Affirmative Testament Chapter A8

Born that Way

Part of the problem LGBT people face in dealing with the churches is that Christian leaders fail to recognise the beautiful diversity of God's children. They hold to a primitive belief that God created everybody heterosexual and that therefore homosexual behaviour is just another sort of wickedness, like robbery and murder, and one which deserves condemnation and punishment, not affirmation and approval.

And they totally ignore the fact that Jesus himself was well aware that some people are not born to marry a person of the opposite sex.

Heterosexual marriage is not for everybody

In the Gospel of Matthew (19: 3-12) Jesus expounds God's view of heterosexual marriage in the course of responding to questions from some Pharisees who were trying to trick him. This passage includes his famous saying that, *'what therefore God hath joined together, let not man put asunder.'*

The Pharisees, thinking they have now 'got' him, then remind Jesus that Moses had permitted men to leave their wives by *'writing a divorcement'*. How could this be if God has ordained marriage to be indissoluble? Jesus answers: *Because of the hardness of your hearts Moses suffered you to put away your wives: but from the beginning it was not so. And I say to you, whoever divorces his wife, except for immorality, and marries another woman commits adultery.*

Hearing this the disciples conclude that *'if the relationship of the man with his wife is like this it must therefore be better not to marry.'*

And this is the point at which Jesus makes clear that heterosexual marriage is definitely not for everybody: *Not all men can accept this teaching, but only those to whom it has been given. For there are eunuchs who were born that way from their mother's womb; and there are eunuchs who were made eunuchs by men; and there are also eunuchs who made themselves eunuchs for the sake of the kingdom of heaven. He who is able to accept this, let him accept it.*

The crucial word here of course is 'eunuch'. If you look the term up in a glossary of the Bible you will read that a eunuch is a chamberlain or official. This is because eunuchs were men who did not have sex with women and/or could not reproduce. They were therefore considered safe to be around women in the harem. And since they had no children, they had no vested interest in leaving wealth to subsequent generations. They could therefore be safely employed in government service without any fear that they would be corrupt or seek to gain advantage for their sons.

Three types of eunuch

Jesus is effectively saying that eunuchs are exempt from the divinely ordained compulsory heterosexual monogamous marriage which applies to everybody else. And he identifies three types of eunuchs to whom this exemption applies:

1. castrated men -*'the eunuchs who are made eunuchs by men'*. These are boys and men whose testicles have been cut off so that they are fit to work in the sensitive official capacities described above.
2. voluntary celibates - *'the eunuchs who make themselves eunuchs for the sake of the kingdom of heaven'* These are devout men who voluntarily abstain from sex with women as part of their religious mission, as Catholic priests are required to do to this day.
3. men who are not interested in sex with women - *'eunuchs who were born that way from their mother's womb'*.

Jesus is not here talking about men with genital deformities. The only realistic conclusion is that he is talking about perfectly normal men with a sexual orientation that is not heterosexual. Prima facie Jesus seems to be acknowledging that homosexuals are an intentional part of God's creation and that they are born that way.

So Christian leaders who condemn lesbian and gay people for their evil lifestyle choice are actually contradicting the teaching of Him in whose name they claim to speak.

Eunuchs in sexual relationships

A further implication of Jesus' use of the term 'eunuch' is that sexual relationships are not ruled out. A eunuch is a man who cannot or does not want to reproduce by having sex with a woman. Eunuch does not mean a man who is not sexual. Indeed some eunuchs were castrated specifically so that they would stay young and pretty and continue to be sexual. Alexander the Great's lover, Bagoas (The Persian Boy), is a famous case in point.

Another example of a eunuch apparently enjoying a sexual relationship with another male is to be found in the book of Daniel in the Old Testament. Right at the beginning of the first chapter of this book we hear of King Nebuchadnezzar, the king of Babylon and his victory over the Kingdom of Judah. Nebuchadnezzar tells Ashpenaz, the master of the eunuchs to select a certain number of the children of Israel to be kept in his palace, and he would supply them with food and drink. Daniel is one of these children but he is defiant and refuses to eat the foreign king's food or drink his wine. He does though establish a good relationship with Ashpenaz: *Now God had brought Daniel into favour and tender love with the prince of eunuchs.* Daniel 1:9

Ashpenaz clearly cares for Daniel, and eventually a deal is negotiated and Daniel's subsequent career in Nebuchadnezzar's court advances rapidly under the eunuch's tutelage.

The 'causes' of homosexuality

Through progress and development in the human and social sciences we have come to understand that being gay is a naturally occurring minority variant, as indeed Jesus' teaching on 'eunuchs born that way from their mother's womb' suggests. It is simply an anthropological fact that homosexuality has existed in all known human societies. The form it takes varies from culture to culture but in no society is it absent. We now also know that this applies in the animal kingdom too. We should therefore not still be having to deal with arguments about gay sex being 'unnatural'. But we do.

When people ask what 'causes' homosexuality you can be pretty sure they are still thinking that heterosexuality is normal and natural, homosexuality is not, and so something must have 'caused it'. Interestingly, this question is mostly asked by straights. Gay people mostly get on with just being who and what they are.

The so-called answers to the question have changed. In earlier times the answer was possession by 'wicked demons' and 'evil spirits' and the remedy was torture and burning alive or some other ghastly end. Or the cause might be put down to your own sinfulness or to the sinfulness of your parents. The remedy was much the same. If you were gay the best you could hope for was being ostracised and rejected by decent society.

In the nineteenth century the answer became medicalised. You were physiologically and/or psychologically disturbed. For the next hundred years or so you would find yourself subjected to all manner of barbaric treatment sensitively and thoughtfully designed to help you move from abnormal gayness to normal straightdom: electric shocks, chemical castration, stringent behaviour modification and the like. This was often instigated against your will by 'caring' agencies such as priests, doctors or your parents, or sometimes forced on you by the courts as an alternative to going to prison. Suicides were common, amongst the most famous and tragic being the case of the brilliant and heroic Alan Turing, the mathematician who broke the German Enigma Code in the Second World War, saving countless lives. He was prosecuted for his homosexuality and sentenced to medical castration which he could not tolerate.

Even now in the twenty-first century the 'ex-gay' ministries are still at it: assuming (wrongly) that homosexuality is not part of God's creation and busily damaging lives through ridiculous and useless 'conversion' programmes of prayer and spiritual 'healing'.

One such ministry, Courage UK, came to understand after almost a decade of trying to 'convert' gay men that it was not only failing but was actually causing a great deal of harm. Courage UK now rescues gay men who have been badly hurt by other so called 'ex gay' ministries. Its director, Jeremy Marks comments: *Towards the end of the 1990s I had become increasingly aware that 'ex-gay' ministries, especially in the USA, were too afraid to assess honestly the fruit of their work and admit their staggering level of failure........ In reality if these people had been running a business that depended for its survival on the quality and reliability of their product, they would have become bankrupt years ago. If they had been offering a medical solution for some sickness or disease and had produced as disastrous a long term effect on their patients as we had, they would have been sued out of existence.* Marks (2008) p.36

Telling the truth in this way was a very brave step which has cost the organisation and its director dear. Unfortunately the vast majority of 'ex gay' ministries have not followed his lead and continue to perpetuate the lie that homosexuality is a sinful disorder which can be 'cured'.

Jesus dismisses the question of 'cause'

Let us be clear: there is absolutely no biblical warrant for any of this.

People used to believe that physical conditions such as being blind, deaf or dumb were caused by evil and sin. In the Gospel of John chapter 9 Jesus and the disciples come across a young man blind from birth. The disciples ask: *Who sinned, this man or his parents, that he was born blind?*

This question reveals clearly the cultural assumptions of the time towards blindness, which sadly are the same cultural assumptions still widespread now about homosexuality. Jesus' reply is very telling. He challenges the assumptions directly: *Neither this man nor his parents sinned; he was born blind so that God's works might be revealed in him.*

For the disciples – the future church – blindness puts this man beyond the pale of godly society and means that he cannot know God and will never enter the kingdom of heaven. But for Jesus this man's blindness, with all its terrible social and religious consequences, does not banish him to the margins but rather puts him at the centre of God's loving concern. Sin has got nothing to do with it. His blindness in itself is simply part of life.

Jesus announces *'I am the light of the* world'. He spits on the ground, *'makes clay of the spittle'* and anoints the eyes of the blind man with it. He tells him to go and wash in the pool of Siloam. On his return the blind man can now see.

This whole process has echoes of baptism. We are all born with original sin – blind from birth – then in the font we are anointed and are thereafter able to 'see', our spiritual vision restored. Very gradually afterwards, through a painful process of realisation, the young man comes to recognise that Jesus is indeed the 'light of the world'. Those around him, however, though they can see, remain blind to this truth. They treat the young man very badly, as if he were socially invisible. He is an embarrassment to his parents both when he was blind and afterwards when he 'comes out' as a self-confident believer in Jesus.

As he is repeatedly interrogated by the Pharisees the young man develops an ever-deepening understanding of Jesus. To begin with he only knows the name, then he says Jesus is a prophet, then he declares he is 'from God', and finally he declares his faith in Jesus as the Son of Man.

Ironically, exactly the reverse process happens with the Pharisees whose attitude hardens as the interrogation progresses. Finally they simply abuse him and throw him out.

At the end of the story Jesus says: *I came into this world for judgement so that those who do not see may see, and those who do see may become blind.*

Jesus in this way completely rejects the question of 'cause'. He takes the meaning of the blindness which the culture of the Pharisees has defined in an oppressive and exclusionary way and reverses it. He does not so much 'cure' the blindness as directly confront the awful social and religious exclusion of blind people in those days. The blind outcast becomes the true believer. It is the Pharisees' own smug self-righteousness and willingness to condemn their fellow men and treat them appallingly that prevents them learning from the outcast. As Jeffrey John comments: *It is a case not so much of 'none so blind as those who will not see' as of 'none so blind as those who are sure they see already.* John (2001) p.136

From these sayings of Jesus we see gay people being just the way they are 'so that's God's works may be revealed' in them. Nobody sinned. It is those who refuse to 'see' this truth who remain in darkness, both literal and metaphoric.

LGBT Self affirmation
Summary Sheet A8: Born that Way

1. In Matthew's Gospel chapter 19 the Pharisees are trying to trick Jesus on the issue of divorce.

2. Jesus forbids divorce but then says that not everybody is able to accept the teaching on marriage because some people are 'eunuchs.'

3. He describes three types of eunuch:
   a. religious people who choose to remain celibate
   b. castrated boys and men who work in the harem
   c. 'eunuchs born that way from their mother's womb'

4. 'Eunuchs born that way' means men whose sexual orientation is not towards women. The implication is that Jesus is here recognising that some men are 'naturally' homosexual.

5. People still ask what 'causes' homosexuality despite the fact that scientific evidence confirms it is just a natural human variant.

6. People used to ask what 'causes' disabilities such as blindness and deafness, and believed it was due to sin.

7. Jesus utterly refutes this idea. He says a young man born blind was born that way 'so that God's works might be revealed in him.' It has nothing to do with sin.

8. After Jesus gives him sight the young man comes to 'see' that Jesus is 'the light of the world'.

9. The Pharisees fail totally to understand that although they have sight they cannot 'see' the truth in front of them.

10. Jeffrey John comments: *'not so much 'none so blind as those will not see' as 'none so blind as those who are sure they see already'.*

The Affirmative Testament Chapter A9

Jesus Was No Family Man

'Family values' as a tool to exclude

During the 1980s Margaret Thatcher's government in Britain introduced anti-gay legislation supposedly to protect 'family values'. As the legislation was passing through the British parliament the author, comedian, and polymath Stephen Fry wrote: *The tenor and thrust of the Legislation (if such a slimy smear swabbed from the epicentre of Satan's anal ring can be dignified with the name) is to criminalise the promotion of homosexuality as an acceptable equivalent of family life. Family life, family values, decent normal family, family fun, family shopping, family leisure. The word is used these days much as the word 'Aryan' was used in Nazi Germany during the 1930s.* Fry (1992) p. 156

The concept of the 'Aryan' was of course designed to divide 'them' (non-German, evil and impure) from 'us' (German, good and pure). A non-Aryan in the Nazi state was a non-person, an 'Untermensch', first excluded, then persecuted, and finally annihilated in the gas ovens of Auschwitz. The concept of 'family values' is used in the same way to divide 'decent normal people like us' from 'deviant perverts like them'. In this chapter we will look at evidence from the Bible to show that Jesus was most definitely not on the side of self righteous 'decent normal people' and was anything but a supporter of 'family values'.

Jesus' opposition to the family

Jesus' attitude to the family is clear, unambiguous and unequivocal. It is one of determined and relentless opposition: *If anyone comes to me and does not hate his own father and mother and wife and children and brothers and sisters and even his own life, that one cannot be my disciple. Whoever does not bear the cross and come after me cannot be my disciple.* Luke 14:26-27

It would be difficult to conceive of a more definitive anti-family statement than this.

'Hate' is just about the strongest term you can use to define your relation to somebody or something. Here's the bottom line: in this text (which is repeated in other gospels) Jesus is telling all those modern day Christian 'family values' evangelisers: you can have your 'family values' or you can have salvation through me. You cannot have both. You choose.

And in a sort of Alice in Wonderland manoeuvre, conservative evangelical Christians have managed to turn Christ's message completely on its head. They say you cannot be saved **unless** you believe in 'family values'. This in fact makes them guilty of idolatry, which St Paul describes as the sin of 'exchanging the truth of God for a lie'. It is a palpable lie that 'family values' have got anything at all to do with salvation and they have exchanged the truth of God as shown by Jesus for this lie. They are effectively worshipping 'family values' in place of God. And worshipping an idea or an idol in the place of God is idolatry.

The complete and utter incompatibility of family ties and Christian discipleship is apparent in Jesus' statement in the Gospel of Luke that: *No one who puts his hand to the plough and then looks back is fit for the reign of God.*

You must leave without saying goodbye and without a single backward glance.

Jesus did not have a family

Jesus' whole life was a living renunciation of 'family values'. He does not marry, he does not have children, and he sees nothing special in his relationship to the people whose blood ties make them relations of his. Shortly after he has chosen the men who will be his disciples the crowd around him tell him that his family have come looking for him: *"Your mother and your brothers and your sisters are outside asking for you.' And he replied, "who are my mother and my brothers?" And looking at those who sat around him, he said, "Here are my mother and my brothers! Whoever does the will of God is my brother and sister and mother".* Mark 3:31-55

The family that matters to Jesus is not his 'family of origin' but rather his 'chosen family' of disciples and others who are committed to working for the Kingdom of God. Willingness to abandon the family of origin was one of the key requirements in the disciples' job description. They too must leave property, work and family commitments behind. But the promise of Jesus is that by so doing they will be rewarded not only with joy and justice in Heaven but with a richer family experience in the here and now. At one point Peter says to Jesus: *"Look, we left everything and have followed you."* Jesus said, *"Truly I say to you, there is no one who left house or mother or father or brothers or sisters or children or fields for my sake and for the sake of the gospel, who does not receive, now in this time, a hundredfold houses and brothers and sisters and mothers and children and lands, with persecutions, and in the coming age life everlasting.* Mark 10:28-30

It is noteworthy that Jesus here links family ties with economic assets and material wealth. And herein lies a clue as to the reasons why he urges rejection of the family. The family is a social and economic structure. Its concerns and drives are all about security, possessions and the transmission of goods and social position from one generation to the next. The family ensnares you in the base interests of this world and prevents you from responding to the love of God and working for his coming kingdom of joyful social justice for all his children. You must extricate yourself from this labyrinth of material distractions and commit yourself body and soul to following Him. If you do this you will find that you have mothers, brothers and sisters galore with whom you will enjoy real fellowship, companionship and mutual trust.

The implication is that there is nothing special about the people you happen to be related to. Even in relation to his own mother Jesus is remarkably detached. On one occasion when Jesus is teaching a woman shouts out to him: *"Blessed is the womb that bore you and the breasts that you sucked!"* But he said, *"blessed rather are those who hear the word of God and keep it"*. Luke 11:27-28

Jesus never addresses Mary as mother, but only ever as 'woman', and he does seem amazingly cool towards her. At the wedding feast in Cana Mary tells Jesus that they have run out of wine. Jesus' response to her is strikingly abrupt, not to say rude and dismissive: *'Woman, what concern is that to you and me?'* John 2:3-4

Similarly, as we have seen in the story of the Beloved Disciple, the only thing Jesus has to say to Mary when he is dying on the cross is: *Woman, behold thy son.* John 19:26

In Jesus' relationship with his biological mother there appears to be not the slightest element of sentimentality. In the gospel accounts we are told that Jesus loved many different people, but we are never told that he loved his mother or that he loved his brothers. Jesus uses the same word to address Mary that he uses in addressing complete strangers, for example the Samaritan woman and the woman taken in adultery. In keeping with Jesus' approach, the great subsequent veneration of Mary in Christian tradition is based as much upon her role as a believer who hears the word of God and acts on it faithfully and loyally, as on her being his birth mother. Although the Church later came to define her as 'the Mother of God', she was not treated in any kind of 'mumsy' way by Jesus during his earthly life.

No fathers: Jesus' opposition to patriarchy

There is an interesting omission in the sayings of Jesus quoted above. Jennings (2003) invites us to notice that the hundredfolds of new relatives you acquire in the new adopted family of Christian disciples does not include fathers. You get mothers, brothers and sisters, but no fathers. Compare this with the first quotation where Jesus lists those relatives you should hate. The hate list most definitely does include fathers. This is not accidental or insignificant.

The point of Jesus' critique of the family is precisely to oppose the patriarchal structures of domination which it supports, antithetical as they are to the values of justice and equality which Jesus has come to proclaim. Christians have only one father, a loving and merciful father, their creator in heaven. By contrast human fathers are the pivot on which all the material and social inequalities of patriarchal traditional societies ultimately rest. In the coming kingdom there will be no fathers: *And call no man your father upon the earth, for one is your Father, which is in heaven.* Matthew 23:9

Jesus is fundamentally against all hierarchies which involve distinctions of power, wealth and status. In the same passage he tells his disciples also not to allow themselves to be called rabbis or masters. The patriarchal system works through just such invidious distinctions. Nobody is to claim a special authority. The first shall be last and the last first.

Once again it is hugely and cruelly ironic that the 'fatherhood of God' has throughout Christian history been used as a religious justification for the very thing that the concept is meant to destroy: patriarchal authority. This is another instance of Christ's message being entirely turned on its head to serve the interests of human greed and lust for power.

Children as the model for discipleship

Jesus' objections to social distinctions are evident also in his attitude to children.

And they were bringing children to him, that he might touch them; and the disciples rebuked them. But Jesus saw it and was furious and said to them, "let the children come to me, don't stop them, for the reign of God belongs to those like them. Truly I say to you, whoever does not receive the reign of God as a child does will not enter it at all." And folding them in his arms, he blesses them laying his hands upon them. Mark10:13-16

The disciples were trying to stop children coming because they were inferior beings, not having the social status of adults, and therefore presumed not yet eligible for entry into the Kingdom. Jesus' frustration at the disciples' inability to understand that he will have no truck with discrimination of any kind is fearfully evident. Far from being inferior, it is the innocence and openheartedness characteristic of children which the 'superior' adults will need to demonstrate if they are to receive salvation.

This commendation of children also clarifies Jesus attitude to children within patriarchal structures. What he is talking about here are children in general who are to be joyously welcomed into the Kingdom of Heaven. In the earlier saying where he urges would-be disciples to leave their children in order to follow him he is talking about children as property, as goods and chattels to serve social and economic purposes. As some commentators have pointed out (e.g. Jennings op.cit.), it is the difference between on the one hand innocent and vulnerable children in need of love and protection and on the other hand 'my' children on whom I project my own social aspirations and economic concerns and whose security I pursue while remaining indifferent to other children. The follower of Jesus is to embrace and care for all children irrespective of biological lineage.

The inevitability of conflict

Jesus' message also carries with it the implication that in the end there may be real conflict involved in being a disciple of his because the renunciation of family and the challenge to patriarchal authority will be bitterly contested.

And brother will deliver up brother to death, and the father his child, and children will rise up against parents and have them put to death; and you will be hated by all for my name's sake. But that which endures to the end will be saved. Mark 13:12-13

Do not think that I have come to bring peace to the earth; I have not come to bring peace but a sword. For I have come to set a man against his father, and a daughter against her mother and a daughter-in-law against her mother-in-law; and one's foes will be members of one's own household.' Matthew 10:34-36

Ultimately, however, all patriarchal hierarchies and social and economic structures are transient and finally the only thing of real lasting substance will be the Kingdom of God.

Good news for LGBT people

Jesus' scathing attack on the family revealed in the analysis of biblical texts above is very good news indeed for LGBT people.

It is very good news twice over.

Firstly, it exposes as totally bogus the claim that by their very existence LGBT people are a 'threat' to Christian family values because there are no Christian family values. It has always been a ridiculous claim that gay people threaten 'marriage and the family'. This is demonising of the worst kind. Heterosexuals are not going to stop marrying each other and producing children because a small percentage of the population is gay. But in these Biblical texts we see that, contrary to what the patriarchal churches teach, Christ was absolutely not an advocate of 'family values'. 'Family values' there may be but 'Christian family values' there are not. The phrase 'family values' essentially denotes a socio-political ideology with which Jesus was clearly not in sympathy.

Secondly, it vindicates and legitimises what so many LGBT people have to do in leaving behind their family of origin to join an adopted family of choice where real fellowship, love and mutual support can be found. These are the Christian values which Christ taught and lived out. His concern was with caring for all not just looking after your own at the expense of others.

In this way, the Jesus of the Bible is a comforting figure for LGBT people. He validates the anxiety many feel about the negative impact of family structures based on biological kinship, and he endorses the ways in which many gay people attempt to retrieve the best aspects of family in the development of relationships grounded in openness, honesty and care. As we shall see in the next chapter, Jesus had no truck with mere compliance with established structures and sought always for an authentic human response to life expressed in heartfelt love of God and neighbour.

LGBT Self affirmation
Summary Sheet A9: Jesus was
No Family Man

1. Jesus makes astonishingly negative statements about the family, going so far as to say anyone who does not hate his family cannot be a disciple of his.

2. Many Christians, especially conservative evangelicals, turn this teaching on its head and imply that you cannot be a disciple of Jesus unless you believe in 'family values'.

3. Jesus did not recognise biological family ties. What mattered to him was not kinship but whether or not people do the will of God – these are his brothers, sisters and mother.

4. By the standard of conservative 'family values' Jesus is remarkably unattached to Mary, whom he never addresses as mother.

5. Jesus challenges patriarchy directly and sees fathers as problematic. He tells his follows to 'call no man your father upon earth'. Only God in Heaven is your Father.

6. Jesus praises the innocence, detachment and openheartedness of children as models for how people should be in order to enter the Kingdom of Heaven.

7. Realising that those with vested material interests in the social structure based on patriarchal families will resist, Jesus predicts inevitable conflict before the Kingdom of Heaven is established on earth.

8. Jesus' teaching on the family is good news for LGBT people who have often suffered as a direct result of so-called 'family values', and who have found refuge in 'families of choice' which resemble Jesus' life with his disciples.

The Affirming Testament Chapter A10

The Pure LGBT Heart

Ritual purity and goodness are not synonymous

As we have seen in earlier discussions of Old Testament texts, the laws and prohibitions of the Torah, the first five books of the Old Testament including Genesis and Leviticus, were specifically intended to separate and distinguish the Jews from their Gentile neighbours and make them a holy people. All the tiny details of the rules and regulations of the Holiness Code, covering every aspect of life from the cradle to the grave, were intended to achieve this one single purpose. The overwhelming concern was with protecting the ritual purity of the Hebrew people, dividing them off from the uncleanness of the nations surrounding them.

But ritual ethnic purity is not synonymous with goodness. And even the Old Testament prophets were aware that there were good people outside Israel amongst the Gentiles who obviously did not follow the rules of holiness and purity. And they also knew that there were Jewish people who did obey all the laws of the Jewish Holiness code but did not behave well and fell away from God's covenant. But nobody highlighted this disjunction between slavish ritual observance on the one hand, and doing good on the other, more starkly than Jesus.

Jesus abolishes the purity laws

Jesus challenged the laws of ritual purity in the Torah very directly. He was not at all concerned with policing the borders of Jewish identity but rather sought to encourage all to respond to the love of God. The dietary laws of the Jewish Holiness Code were an irrelevance in his eyes. For him it did not matter what you put into your mouth. What matters is what comes out through the words in your mouth from your heart and your mind: *It is not what goes into the mouth that defiles a person but it is what comes out which defiles.... What comes out of the mouth proceeds from the heart, and this is what defiles. For out of the heart come evil intentions, murder, adultery, fornication, theft, false witness, slander. These are what defile a person. But to eat with unwashed hands does not defile.* Matthew 15:17-20

This would have sounded scandalous and shocking to devout Jews at the time. But Jesus was scathing about the pious who paraded their compliance with the laws for external show. What he valued was not ritual purity but purity of heart. He quotes the Old Testament prophet, Isaiah, who generations before had condemned those who publicly, assiduously and ostentatiously observe the purity laws but harbour malignity in their depths: *Well hath Isaiah prophesied of you hypocrites, as it is written, 'This people honoureth me with their lips, but their heart is far from me'.*

External compliance with a set of rules has nothing to do with inner virtue.

Oral Sex

It is possible to read Jesus' comments here as going far beyond the simple issue of food and eating, perhaps even to include the issue of oral sex.

Unlike the Pharisees, Jesus is clearly not just talking about food. He has expanded the discussion to get literally to the heart of the matter. Jesus is saying that all these laws and rules are of no consequences unless they ensure purity of heart. Interpreted literally they themselves cannot define what is 'clean' and 'unclean'. What is 'clean' is love of God and love of neighbour. What is 'unclean' is hate and evil intentions. What you do or do not put into your mouth has nothing to do with it. In this perspective, the cleanness or uncleanness of an act of oral sex would not be established by the mere act itself, but rather the intentions behind it. If it was an act of love it would be clean; if it was an act of lust, force or violence it would be unclean. This strongly suggests that Jesus did not see two gay men or two gay women expressing their love in acts of oral sex as sinful. Here then is another of the sayings of Jesus which the patriarchal Christian churches have been slow properly to understand.

Waiting for Peter

Even in the time of the apostles it took a while for the disciples and the early Church to grasp the immediate implications of Jesus' teaching. Even Peter, the Rock on whom the Church was to be founded, did not initially understand how radical Jesus' rejection of the Jewish law actually was. Not until later do we read that in a dream Peter saw: *The heaven opened, and something like a large sheet coming down, being lowered to the ground by its four corners. In it were all kinds of four footed creatures and reptiles and birds of the air. Then he heard a voice saying, 'get up Peter, kill and eat'. But Peter said, 'by no means Lord; for I have never eaten anything that is profane or unclean'. The voice said to him again, a second time, 'what God has made clean, you must not call profane.'* Acts 10: 11-15

Only at this point does Peter begin to comprehend the magnitude of the change which Jesus has ushered in. For him this was a total paradigm shift involving three literally world-shattering transformations:

(1) Jewish purity laws no longer apply because everything which God has made is good;
(2) Jewish purity laws no longer apply because to be a rule-obeying Jew does not make you a good person in God's eyes;
(3) Jewish purity laws no longer apply because they only define what it is to be a Jew, which from the point of view of salvation is now irrelevant since God's Kingdom is being extended to embrace all of humanity.

Peter then realises that: *God has shown me that I should not call anyone profane or unclean.* Acts 10:28

and

I truly understand that God shows no partiality, but in every nation anyone who fears God and does what is right is acceptable to God. Acts 10:34

Henceforth there are no more clean and unclean nations. Every individual who loves God and neighbour with a pure heart is clean and belongs in the Kingdom of Heaven.

The baptism of Cornelius

Some other people in the early church, especially the Jewish converts, had difficulty absorbing these ideas. Matters came to a head when they started demanding that Gentile believers in Jesus should be circumcised according to the ritual purity laws. Peter patiently explains the significance of Jesus' teaching to them during a heated discussion reported in Acts chapter 15, and succeeds in getting the Council of Apostles and Elders to decide to abolish this iconic rule in the Leviticus Holiness code.

In his epistle to the Galatians Paul develops the implications of this decision: *For in Christ Jesus neither circumcision nor uncircumcision counts for anything; the only thing that counts is faith working through love.* Galatians 5:6

The abolition of the Jewish law and emphasis on evidence of the Holy Spirit working through the lives of individuals mean that anyone pure in heart could be welcomed into God's Kingdom. In Acts chapter 10 we read that Peter's dream enabled him to baptize Cornelius, a roman centurion, into the Church. For many of Peter's contemporaries this was seriously alarming. Here was not just a Gentile, but a powerful Roman leader of the hated army occupying and oppressing Israel, becoming part of 'their' divine kingdom. But for Peter, now, none of this mattered. There was clear evidence of the working of the Holy Spirit in Cornelius' life and he was pure in heart. Therefore he says: *can any man forbid water, that these should not be baptised, which have received the Holy Spirit as we?* Acts 10:47

Cornelius and the Gentiles had to wait some time for Peter but once understanding dawned the change came quickly and wholeheartedly.

The pure LGBT heart still waiting for Peter now

So from now on the issue is not compliance with the Jewish Holiness code but an authentic responding to God's love and a willing embracing of his Holy Spirit. Anyone can be welcomed into the Church who is pure in heart. There are no 'clean' and 'unclean' people any more. As Paul wrote: *I am persuaded in the Lord Jesus that nothing is unclean in itself.* Romans 14:14

Jesus, Peter and Paul all reject the Holiness Code as a requirement for salvation. Hence Christians are free to eat shrimps and pork, to wear mixed fibres and to tolerate their disobedient sons without killing them. By the same logic they are also freed from the prohibition on lying 'the lyings of a woman' because it is overthrown along with the whole code of purity of which it is a part. This is in effect the consignment to the dustbin of history of the only prohibition in the whole of the Bible that can be said to apply explicitly to male-male sexual intercourse. It should have been the end of anti-gay religious teaching. Unfortunately, as we know, it was not.

James Alison (2003) has pointed out the striking parallel between the situation of the Gentiles then and LGBT Christians now. Peter assumed for a long time that Jesus' message was only for Jews and the only way for Gentiles to become part of it was to repent of their Gentileness, undergo circumcision, and become Jewish. Gentiles like Cornelius accepted this because they could not shake off the idea that something was calling them. They lived with their position as 'half insiders, half outsiders'. And then Peter has his dream, which is in many ways even more dramatic in its effect than the better known Damascene conversion of Paul. And suddenly, Alison suggests, Peter and the disciples experience: *the dawning realisation that God likes the impure people, that God wants them to be on the inside of God's story..... God is not confronting them to get them to repent, or even inviting them to become something else. God is possessing them with delight, and they are delighting in the being possessed.* (Alison (2003) Introduction page x)

As a result, the whole distinction between 'pure' and 'impure' collapses and disappears. A brand new and previously impossible story starts to be told. Those who were earlier excluded are now included and everyone has to begin to work out what the implications of this development are.

Alison's argument is that LGBT people are still in the position of 'waiting for Peter'. Cornelius is in a real sense the prototype of gay Christians. At the moment the only official option open to homosexual Christians is to walk alongside the Church as an impure outsider as Cornelius did, recognising that only by doing the impossible thing of 'repenting' of being homosexual is insider status possible. More and more, however, gay Christians are not doing this impossible thing any more and are living openly as if they were already insiders, and as if they were already an integral part of the Christian story in which God loves all his Children, not just the heterosexual ones. Increasingly, straight Christians are coming to understand that the story gay Christians are telling is their story as well and that the gay/straight distinction means no more to God than the Gentile/Jew distinction. In the first century AD Gentiles had to 'wait for Peter' to realise that they were insiders. Two thousand years later in the twenty-first century AD, LGBT people are doing exactly the same thing, still waiting for Peter. Alison's view is that 'Peter' as a proxy for the leaders of the mainstream churches is beginning to understand, the taboo is disintegrating, and the old exclusionism is finished. Nevertheless it may take a little time yet.

LGBT Self affirmation
Summary Sheet A10: The Pure LGBT Heart

1. Even in the Old Testament people understood that ritual purity and human goodness were not synonymous.

2. Jesus specifically abolished the purity laws for his followers in arguing that what goes into the mouth does not defile a person. It is what comes out of the mouth in terms of evil intentions that defiles. What he valued was purity of heart not ritual purity.

3. The disciples took a long time to understand this. Peter has a dream in which he is told to eat animals the purity laws define as unclean and realises that God has not made anything unclean.

4. Peter still faced resistance from Jewish converts who wanted to circumcise all Christ's followers.

5. Matters come to a head over the case of Cornelius, a Roman centurion whom Peter baptises because all that is important is that he has clearly received the Holy Spirit.

6. The overthrowing of the Holiness Code implies the abolition of the prohibition of male-male intercourse in Leviticus.

7. As James Alison has pointed out, this means that God is welcoming LGBT people into his church without condition or repentance but for who they are as they are, just as Peter eventually understood that the Gentiles were to be welcomed.

8. Currently the mainstream churches continue to resist this implication and pure in heart LGBT people are in this sense still 'waiting for Peter'.

The Affirmative Testament Chapter A11

The Transgendering Christ

The implications of Jesus' being 'fully human'

During the chapters of the Affirmative Testament there have been a number of occasions where it has been important to stress that Jesus was fully human. It took the Church many centuries to arrive at the definitive doctrine that he was simultaneously both divine and human. Claims that he was either human and not fully divine, or divine and not fully human, were eventually deemed heretical. However the churches, as discussed in these earlier chapters, have nevertheless been reluctant to face up to the real implications of Jesus' being fully human. They really have not wanted to consider what it meant for him to be gendered and sexualised.

One particular aspect of Jesus' being fully human, which by and large the Christian churches have completely ignored, is how his humanity embraced both the male and the female. Jesus makes it abundantly clear in his teaching and his actions that his mission is to offer salvation to everybody. And everybody means women as well as men. As we have seen, in much of the Old Testament women are all but invisible and simply do not count. One might even doubt whether the authors of some of the books of the Old Testament considered women to be 'fully human'! By contrast Jesus goes out of his way to affirm the equal worth of women. In this sense he is the universal human saviour who understands fully what it is to be a human male and a human female.

Transcending gender

Some commentators have drawn the conclusion that in order to discharge this universal mission Christ must in some sense have transcended gender, embodying within himself the constituent elements of both masculinity and femininity. The remarkable nineteenth century preacher, F.W. Robertson, argued that Jesus literally incorporated both genders: *One there was in whom human nature was exhibited in all its elements symmetrically complete. One in whom there met all that was manliest and all that was most womanly.*

Quoting the famous passage in St Paul's letter to the Galatians (3:28) about there being in Christ neither Jew nor Greek, bond nor free, male or female, he comments: *That is the other thing implied in His title to the Son of Man. His nature had in it the nature of all nations: but also His heart had in it the blended qualities of both sexes.*

Robertson is at pains to emphasise that the phrase Son of Man actually means Son of Humanity. The Biblical language uses 'man' here in the sense of 'mankind' covering both males and females: *When the Bible tells us Jesus Christ was the Son of Man it uses the word which implies human being: it does not use the word which signifies one of the male sex; it does not dwell on the fact that He was a man: but it earnestly asserts that He was Man.*

The incarnation, Jesus as the 'word made flesh' as St John puts it, is of ultimate significance for all humanity, and therefore the scriptural stress has to be on his being a human, not on his being a man. Therefore what we should look for is the integration of masculine and feminine qualities in Jesus' character.

Christ is firm, unconquerable, true to the cause of God and man, but also loving, tender, gentle. Choose that type. He is the one model, the one type.

From this theological position Robertson argues that men should seek to acquire feminine virtues so that 'the whole of Christ may be formed in them', although interestingly he does not urge women to develop masculine virtues. It is as if he thinks it is the masculine which is more problematic. In another sermon he declares: *The glory of true womanhood consists in being herself:*

not in striving to be something else. It is the false paradox and heresy of this present age to claim for her as a glory the right to leave her sphere.

What Robertson is concerned with is the reconciliation of masculine and feminine values. He seems to be saying that being conciliatory is already a feminine quality but one which males need to learn. Only Christ is fully able to integrate these qualities perfectly: *Christ is the realised idea of our Humanity. He is God's idea of Man completed.* (All the above Robertson extracts are quoted in Beardsley (2009) ps 292-293)

As Beardsley comments, Robertson describes: *a Romantic Christ who combines the best of masculine and feminine qualities, and transcends male and female. A perfect embodiment of the gender blending that he believed was characteristic of all great poets and artists, Robertson's Christ, strong, yet tender, true yet sympathetic.....* Beardsley op.cit. p. 307

The equality of the female and the male

Others have been more explicit about the emancipatory implications of a transgendered incarnation in the person of Jesus Christ. For the strikingly named 19th century clergyman, Carteret John Halford Fletcher, who was a City Lecturer and Rector of St Martin's Church in Oxford it meant directly confronting traditional church teaching on gender roles. Seemingly several decades in advance of his times, Fletcher challenged the subordinate position of women based on the comparison with Eve. The transgendered Christ comes in this sense as a female liberator: *Women's original equality with Man is recovered in Christ. The true ground of her restored dignity is often misrepresented. It does not rest on the fact that the Virgin Mary was the divinely selected instrument of the Incarnation... Nor is it Woman's elevation in Christ derived from her relation as Wife being (according to St Paul) a sacramental sign of the church's relation to Christ. Its true cause lies deeper. It is found, first, in this, that Christ's character manifested the womanly virtues – purity, sympathy, gentleness, obedience – which had died out of the world with Woman's degradation. You must never forget that Christ is neither Man nor Woman. He is the divine likeness, the whole humanity. Manhood and Womanhood in one.* (Quoted in Johnson (1983) p.144)

Contemporary western cultures have now institutionalised equality between the sexes, at least in principle. Gender equality is a more or less universal value in secular society, although actual practice may lag somewhat behind. Perversely, however, the patriarchal churches seem in many cases to have adopted an even harder line on the subordinate position of women, possibly as a reaction to the advancement of female emancipation. Robertson and Fletcher's admonitions are still needed, as is a more widespread understanding of the scriptural texts which justify them, some of which they cannot actually have known about.

The scriptural context

Scholars have long known of the existence of a gospel written by St Thomas through references in other documents, but an actual copy was only discovered in 1945 as part of a library of scrolls which came to light in Egypt at Nag Hammadi.

This Gospel is very important for LGBT people. Researchers now believe that it is as reliable a source for the original forms of the sayings of Jesus as the existing four. This is particularly significant when what Jesus says challenges patriarchy and hierarchy.

Thomas reports the following exchange between Peter and Jesus: *Simon Peter said to them, 'Let Mary (Magdalene) leave us, for women are not worthy of life'.*

Jesus said, 'I myself shall lead her in order to make her male, so that she too may become a living spirit resembling you males. For every woman who will make herself male will enter the kingdom of heaven'. (Saying no 114)

What we are dealing with here is Mary Magdalene being

entrusted with the male work of proclaiming the gospel after Jesus' resurrection. It may look at first sight as if Jesus is reinforcing the privileges of males, but his intention is the very opposite. Mary is to become male only in the sense of being given the freedom of discipleship, releasing her from the restrictions of the female role and 'women's work'.

The recent discussion in the General Synod of the Church of England about whether women can become bishops appears to have rerun exactly this exchange 2000 years later. The dismay of Peter then, and the dismay of traditionalist conservative males in the Church now, look much the same. They are all males seeking to guard their privileges.

In the Gospel of Thomas Jesus is specifically reported as counselling subversion of the traditional gender roles. In an earlier saying Jesus declares: *When you make the two one....and when you make the male and the female one and the same, so that the male will not be male nor the female female...then you will enter the kingdom. (Saying no 22)*

There can be no doubt that assertions like these directly challenge the sexual and gender laws of the Old Testament and show Jesus as a sexual liberator. Even Paul, whose writings are often used to keep women 'in their place' and to condemn homosexuals, nevertheless found himself writing: *in Christ there is no male or female...you are all one in Christ Jesus.* Galations 3:28

And there are further indications of a transgender approach in the other gospels. In preparing to celebrate the Passover which will become his last supper Jesus sends ahead two of his disciples telling them: *a man carrying a jar of water will meet you; follow him.* Mark 14:13, Luke 22:10

Nothing extraordinary here you might think. The point is though that men did not carry water in those days. Gender roles then were strictly separated and this was women's work. As Jennings (2003) has pointed out, this is like Jesus saying, 'look out for a man wearing lipstick'. Here is a person flouting the norms of gender behaviour who will act as the guide to a place of safety for Jesus and the disciples, who themselves transgressed the established religious and social customs of orthodox respectability. In short, this is Jesus working with and drawing into the kingdom the equivalent in today's terms of a trans-vestite.

More outrageously the gospel of John tells us that just before the Last Supper, Jesus himself took on 'women's work'. He *got up from the table, took of his clothes, and tied a towel around himself. Then he poured water into a basin and began to wash the disciples' feet and to wipe them with the towel that was tied around him.* John 13:4-5

For men in that era this was truly shocking. Peter objects but Jesus answers: *You do not know now what I am doing but later you will understand............Unless I wash you, you will have no share with me.* John 13: 7

It is generally believed that this is a supreme act of humility by Jesus, but this is not stated in the text. Nor does that argument really make any sense. What Jesus actually does is to act not as a slave but as a woman. In every other instance in the Bible anyone who washes somebody else's feet is always a woman, as was required by the normative conventions of the time.

Furthermore Jesus commands all his follows to commemorate him in the same way through this act of transgressing gender categories: *So if I, your Lord and teacher, have washed your feet, you also ought to wash one another's feet. For I have set you an example, that you should also do as I have done to you.* John 13:14-15

As Jennings notes, this commandment comes at the point where Jesus is most acutely aware of who he is and where he is going. It is through transcending the most rigorously enforced institutions of earthly society, gender role expectations, that he expresses his 'divine' identity. And he seems to call on all of us also to disregard gender identity in order to realise the fullness of our baptism as God's children, *'concerning whom the world knows neither from whence they come nor whither they go'.*

Queer theory the way forward?

It is cruelly ironic that two thousand years later the patriarchal churches have made Christianity the ultimate conservative bastion of gender role conformity. For if the truth is that in Christ there really is no male or female, the current anti-women and anti-gay stance of so many of these churches puts them in direct conflict with the will of God as expressed in the teachings of Jesus cited throughout the chapters of this book's Affirmative Testament. If the concept of gender is to be dissolved in the Kingdom of Heaven, then ipso facto any discrimination based on sexual orientation collapses with it. In today's terminology we might therefore equally say that in Christ there is no gay or straight for we are all one in Christ Jesus. In fact the full implication is that the universal transgendering Christ dissolves all social distinctions and draws all those who believe to himself.

It is for this reason that some commentators see the way forward in the future for LGBT people in their struggle against ecclesiastical condemnation as lying in queer theology based on queer theory which renders all social distinctions problematic. All these distinctions, gender, class, ethnicity, age, sexual orientation, disability and the identities they produce are socially constructed. The programme of queer theorists is to relativize and deconstruct them in order to show how 'ultimately' they are meaningless because they only have form and validity in relation to a given socio-cultural context. All socio-cultural contexts are temporary and transient, and therefore there is no 'ultimate' reality in any of the social category definitions and identities they create. We have already seen for example how the social construction of homosexuality was quite different in Ancient Greece, or that there was no concept of 'the homosexual' in Western Europe much before the nineteenth century. Just think how irrelevant the social category definitions of feudal society are to us now. Being a 'knight' or a 'serf' for example is literally meaningless in modern western societies; in this socio-cultural context there are no such things. The logic of the argument advanced by queer theorists is that the same will be true in the future for identities we take seriously now.

In relation to gender categories, Josephine Butler (1990) has argued that role definitions of male and female are sustained through repeated 'performances' and that the way to unmask their constructed and relative character is to 'make trouble' and perform them with critical difference. Stuart (1993) has suggested that what this amounts to is parodying them. 'Camp' and 'drag' for example are clear instances of gender role parody, where the manner in which male and female identities are constructed is laid bare and so rendered problematic. This is liberating in the sense that by virtue of this parody we can all see that something we are urged to regard as a 'given' of hard reality to which we have to conform ourselves is no such thing, but is actually manufactured in and through culturally contextualised social interaction. And therefore if it oppresses us we no longer need to suffer. Rather than suffer, we can subvert.

Stuart (op.cit p.108) shows how in religious traditions there is a long history of parodying gender and the assumed normality of relations between the sexes. She points out that monks, for example, have always been living testaments to two important facts:

(1) that Christian discipleship does not require obedience to the rule of compulsory heterosexual marriage and family life;
(2) that all desire is ultimately oriented towards God.

In the monasteries and convents gender definitions were relatively fluid, with religious women often being known by masculine names, and religious men wearing garments which look like female apparel. And as we have seen, some of Jesus' actions and teaching could be interpreted in Butler's terms as making gender trouble.

The question then arises of whether there is any ultimate identity at all? Stuart is very clear that our ultimate identity is our baptismal identity. At our baptism we are given an identity for eternity as sheer gratuitous gift. It is quite outside the normal processes of identity creation through social negotiation by means of which we get all our other senses of self. And at our death it will be the only identity left. All else will have 'withered and perished' as the hymn writer has it. Stuart comments: *It is not that the baptised are called to live beyond culture, which is impossible and undesirable because the Spirit is active in human culture, but that they are called to transform it by living in it in such a way as to testify to the other world being born within it. All our cultural identities are placed under eschatological erasure. Heterosexuality and homosexuality and maleness and femaleness are not of absolute importance, they are not determinative in God's eyes and in so far as any of us have behaved as if they are grounds upon which to exclude people from the glorious liberty of the children of God we are guilty of profanity and a fundamental denial of our own baptismal identity, which rests in being bound together with others not of our choosing by an act of sheer grace.* Stuart (1993) p 107.

Jesus was thus arguably the first queer theorist. He constantly focused on his identity within the Kingdom of Heaven and performed with very critical differences all the social roles into which he was conscripted by the culture of his time, including gender, as we have seen above. For LGBT people therefore his invitation to 'follow me' in this regard is one that can and should be accepted readily with joy, hope and confidence.

LGBT Self affirmation
Summary Sheet A11: The Transgendering Christ

1. The Christian churches teach that Jesus was fully human as well as being fully divine. They are, however, reluctant to recognise the implications of his being fully human and therefore sexual.

2. Jesus' teaching is clear: salvation is for all of humanity. Women are of equal worth. His incarnation as a human being therefore means embracing both male and female.

3. Several commentators have argued that Christ thus necessarily transcended gender and liberates women from the subordinate position to which patriarchal societies confine them.

4. The Gospel of Thomas, a copy of which came to light in 1945, contains explicit sayings of Jesus about the irrelevance of gender.

5. There are also transgender implications in two stories involving Jesus directly:
   a. the water carrier
   b. washing the disciples' feet

6. Two disciples are told to meet a man carrying a jar of water who will show them the secret location for the Passover meal. Only women carried water in those days.

7. The disciples are shocked when Jesus insists on washing their feet. This is not because it is an act of humility but because it is a female act.

8. Jesus tells the disciples to do as he has done, i.e. effectively to transcend gender stereotypes.

9. St Paul's famous statement that 'in Christ there is no male or female' can in this context equally be said to imply that in Christ there is no gay or straight.

10. Ultimately Christ transcends not only gender categories but every social distinction in drawing all to himself.

11. Queer theorists believe LGBT people should 'make trouble' by performing gender roles with critical difference to reveal their relative and arbitrary nature.

12. Ultimately all social identities are temporary and transient. Only baptismal identity endures.

The Affirmative Testament Chapter A12

Conclusion and Final Affirmation

The present book has sought to demonstrate three realities:

(1) nowhere does the Bible condemn same sex love;
(2) LGBT lives, identities and relationships are affirmed in the Bible;
(3) the anti-gay teachings of patriarchal churches are based on prejudice, not on the Bible.

There are very few texts in the Bible that anybody could possibly think have anything remotely to do with homosexuality. Yet we hear about them all the time. On the other hand there are many long and quite unequivocal pro-gay passages in the Bible, the 'plain sense' of which the Church chooses to ignore. Consider just two different issues by way of illustration: slavery and usury.

There are many passages in support of slavery which the Church upheld for centuries but now feels free to disregard (e.g. Ephesians 6:5-9; Colossians 3: 22-4:1; Timothy 6:1-2; 1 Peter 2:1). When did you last here a Church leader call for the reintroduction of slavery in the name of Scriptural authority?

The Christian churches are not supposed to make use of banks and investments to make profits because the Bible expressly forbids usury and the taking of interest. But churches ignore the Bible and do this all the time (e.g. Exodus 22:25; Psalm 15:15; Proverbs 28:8; Ezekial 18:13, 17, 22:12). Have you seen Christians protesting outside banks about the evils of usury recently?

How is it possible that the 'Bible believing' churches can ignore teachings such as these and others on a host of subjects, many of which Jesus Himself gave, while at the same time insisting on the supposed letter of the law in a handful of ambiguous texts on a subject about which Jesus said nothing at all?

The answer, I suspect, is to be found with Alice, in Wonderland, in the mouth of that most celebrated of all textual abusers, Humpty Dumpty. His response to Alice's question in *Through the Looking Glass* seems to give us the key to so many church 'pastoral documents':

> *I don't know what you mean by 'glory', Alice said.*
>
> *Humpty Dumpty smiled contemptuously. Of course you don't – till I tell you. I meant "there's a nice knock-down argument for you!"*
>
> *But 'glory' doesn't mean "a nice knock-down argument", Alice objected.*
>
> *When I use a word, Humpty Dumpty said in a rather scornful tone, 'it means just what I choose it to mean – neither more nor less.*
>
> *The question is, said Alice, whether you **can** make words mean so many different things.*
>
> *The question is, said Humpty Dumpty, which is to be master – that's all.*

For the patriarchal Christian churches the texts discussed in the Defensive Testament will mean whatever they want them to mean. As we have seen, the story of Sodom is actually about hospitality and foreshadows Jesus' commandment to love your neighbour, Leviticus is about ritual purity and preserving male domination. And St Paul is about idolatry. But for the patriarchal churches they are all about condemning gay people.

In a similar way, these churches remain in denial about what is there in the Bible for anyone to see: passages and stories which affirm gay people. There is for example Samuel's account of the love of David and Jonathan, there is the whole Book of Ruth which is about the undying love of two women for each other, and there is the gay centurion who loves his male servant so much he takes enormous risks to get him cured. But for the patriarchal churches, of course, none of them are gay.

And when it comes to Jesus himself these churches batten down the hatches totally. Fully human he might be but they cannot bring themselves to see his sexuality. And yet St John's Gospel gives us a clear account of an astonishingly strong loving relationship between Jesus and a disciple whose only role in the narrative is to be his beloved. Throughout the centuries scholars have understood this to be a homoerotic partnership. Even more striking is the way in which the patriarchal churches have not only misrepresented Jesus' teaching but actually turned it on its head. Jesus hated families but now is portrayed as the divine proponent of 'family values'. Jesus argued against gender stereotyping but these churches now are the last bastion of gender discrimination. Jesus included outcasts and the marginalised in the Kingdom of Heaven but these churches still practise exclusion. The list goes on.

Mark Jordan has suggested that the patriarchal churches actually are not so much interested in defending their arguments as simply asserting again and again their own pernicious ideologies, which he calls 'instruments of power'. As the marketing and advertising industries are well aware, all you need to do to persuade people of something is to say it over and over and over again. This endless repetition carries with it an aura of magisterial authority as though it were obviously so and therefore pointless to argue. And this is the real intention: to shut down any debate. Jordan's advice therefore is: *Responding to ideological discourse requires a rule, not just of suspicion, but of inversion: we should attend not to what the discourse says, but to how it operates.* Jordan (2002) p 151

It is therefore important for LGBT people to know and understand what Jesus actually did and said because the assertion of

Christian leaders that the Bible condemns homosexuality is too often simply taken at face value, when actually this is mere ideological propaganda, as Jordan suggests. These leaders exploit the unfamiliarity of the general public with Biblical texts and the debates surrounding their interpretation. LGBT people need to be able to point up the inadequacies in the arguments of Christian homophobes. They need also to assert with confidence that they are as much numbered amongst God's children as anybody else. If this book has made any small contribution to facilitating such defence and affirmation its purpose will have been achieved.

Visit www.thegaygospels.com

Select Bibliography

Ackroyd, P (1971) The First Book of Samuel, Cambridge, Cambridge University Press

Alison, J (2003) On Being Liked, London, Darton, Longman and Todd

Alison, J (2010) Broken Hearts New Creations: Intimations of a Great Reversal, London, Darton, Longman and Todd

Beardsley, C (2009) Unutterable Love, Cambridge, Lutterworth Press

Boswell, J (1980) Christianity, Social Tolerance and Homosexuality: Gay People in Western Europe form the Beginning of the Christian Era to the Fourteenth Century, Chicago Press

Bates, S (2004) A Church At War, London, IB Tauris

Boswell, J (1994) Same-Sex Unions in Premodern Europe, New York, Villard Books

Brooten, BJ (1996) Love Between Women: Early Christian Responses to Female Homoeroticism, University of Chicago Press

Butler, J (1990) Gender Trouble: Feminism and the Subversion of Identity, London, Routledge

Church of England House of Bishops (2003) Issues in Human Sexuality: A Guide to the Debate, Church House Publishing

Comstock, GD (1993) Gay Theology Without Apology, Cleveland, The Pilgrim Press

Countryman, LW (1988) Dirt, Greed and Sex: Sexual Ethics in the New Testament and their Implications for Today, Philadelphia, Fortress Press

Congregation for the Doctrine of the Faith (1986) Letter to the Bishops of the Catholic Church on the Pastoral Care of Homosexual Persons, London, Catholic Truth Society

Evangelical Alliance (1999) Faith, Hope and Homosexuality

Fry, S (1993) Paperweight, London, Heinemann

Furnish, VP (1979) Homosexuality. In the Moral Teaching of Paul Nashville: Abingdon Press, pages 52-83

Goss, R (1993) Jesus Acted Up: A Gay and Lesbian Manifesto, Harper San Francisco

Groddeck, GW The Book of the It, New York, Vintage Press

Hanway, DG (2006) A Theology of Lesbian and Gay Inclusion, London, Haworth Press

Hare, J (2007) 'Neither Male or Female': the case of intersexuality, in Dormor, D and Morris, J (Eds) An Acceptable Sacrifice? Homosexuality and the Church, London, SPCK

Helminiak, D (2000) What the Bible Really Says about Homosexuality, Alamo Square Press

Hollenbach, P (1981) 'Jesus, Demoniacs, and Public Authorities: A Socio-historical Study,' Journal of the American Academy of Religion 49 (1981) p 573

Horner, T (1978) Jonathan Loved David: Homosexuality in Biblical Times, Philadephia, Westminster Press.

Jennings, T W (2003) The Man Jesus Loved, Cleveland, The Pilgrim Press

Jennings, T W (2009) Jacob's Wound: Homoerotic Narratives in the Literature of Ancient Israel, Cleveland, The Pilgrim Press

John, J (2001) The Meaning in the Miracles, Norwich, Canterbury Press

John, J (1993) 'Permanent, Faithful, Stable' London, Darton, Longman and Todd

Johnson, DA (1983) Women in English Religion 1700-1925 New York and Toronto, Edwin Mellon Press

Jordan, M (2000) The Silence of Sodom: Homosexuality in Modern Catholicism, University of Chicago Press

Jordan, M (2002) The Ethics of Sex , Oxford, Blackwell

Loughlin, G (2007) Queer Theology: Rethinking the Western Body, London, Wiley Blackwell

Marks, J (2008) Exchanging the Truth of God for a Lie, London,

Courage UK

Martin, D (2006) Sex and the Single Saviour, Westminster, John Knox Press

McNeil, J (1976) The Church and the Homosexual, London, Darton, Longman and Todd

McNeil, J (1988) Taking a Chance on God, Boston, Beacon Press

McNeil, J (1995) Freedom, Glorious Freedom, Boston, Beacon Press

Moore, G (2003) A Question of Truth, London and New York, Continuum

Scroggs, R (1983) Homosexuality in the New Testament: Contextual Background for Contemporary Debate, Philadelphia, Fortress Press

Stuart, E (2003) Gay and Lesbian Theologies: Repetitions with Critical Difference, Aldershot, Aldgate Press

Thatcher, A (2008) The Savage Text, Oxford, Wiley Blackwell

Trible, P (2003) Texts of Terror, London SCM Press

Vasey, M (1995) Strangers and Friends: A New Exploration of Homosexuality and the Bible, London, Hodder and Stoughton

Veyne, P (1985) Homosexuality in Ancient Rome, in Aries and Bejin (Eds) Western Sexuality, Blackwell, Oxford

Wilson, N (1995) Our Tribe: Queer Folks, God, Jesus and the Bible, Harper San Francisco

BOOKS

O is a symbol of the world, of oneness and unity. In different cultures it also means the "eye," symbolizing knowledge and insight. We aim to publish books that are accessible, constructive and that challenge accepted opinion, both that of academia and the "moral majority."

Our books are available in all good English language bookstores worldwide. If you don't see the book on the shelves ask the bookstore to order it for you, quoting the ISBN number and title. Alternatively you can order online (all major online retail sites carry our titles) or contact the distributor in the relevant country, listed on the copyright page.

See our website **www.o-books.net** for a full list of over 500 titles, growing by 100 a year.

And tune in to myspiritradio.com for our book review radio show, hosted by June-Elleni Laine, where you can listen to the authors discussing their books.